DATE DUE

Teen Runaways

Teen Runaways

Look for these and other books in the Lucent Overview Series:

Teen Addiction
Teen Alcoholism
Teen Depression
Teen Dropouts
Teen Eating Disorders
Teen Parenting
Teen Pregnancy
Teen Prostitution
Teen Rape
Teens and Divorce
Teens and Drunk Driving
Teen Sexuality
Teen Smoking
Teen Suicide
Teen Violence

Teen Runaways

by Christina Veladota

TEEN ISSUES

LUCENT
BOOKS

THOMSON

™

GALE

San Diego • Detroit • New York • San Francisco • Cleveland • New Haven, Conn. • Waterville, Maine • London • Munich

For more information, contact
Lucent Books
27500 Drake Rd.
Farmington Hills, MI 48331-3535
Or you can visit our Internet site at http://www.gale.com

LIBRARY OF CONGRESS CATALOGING-IN-PUBLICATION DATA

Veladota, Christina.
    Teen runaways / by Christina Veladota.
        p. cm. — (Teen issues)
Includes bibliographical references and index.
    ISBN 1-56006-780-2 (hardback : alk. paper)
    1. Runaway teenagers—Juvenile literature. I. Title. II. Lucent overview series.
Teen issues.
    HV1421.V45 2004
    362.74—dc21

                                                        2003002057

Printed in the United States of America

Contents

INTRODUCTION   8

CHAPTER ONE   12
Who Are Teen Runaways and Why Do They Run?

CHAPTER TWO   23
Life on the Streets

CHAPTER THREE   38
Runaways Face Serious Health Risks

CHAPTER FOUR   49
Runaways and the Law

CHAPTER FIVE   62
Help for Runaways

CHAPTER SIX   74
Alternatives and Prevention

NOTES   87
ORGANIZATIONS TO CONTACT   93
FOR FURTHER READING   97
WORKS CONSULTED   99
INDEX   105
PICTURE CREDITS   111
ABOUT THE AUTHOR   112

Introduction

FOR ALMOST EVERY person, the teen years can be a difficult time. School, social and extracurricular activities, jobs, and responsibilities in the home can make the average adolescent's life hectic and overwhelming. For teen runaways, however, these problems seem insignificant. Rather than worrying about keeping up their grades in school or doing their chores at home, teens on the run must concern themselves daily with finding food and shelter. Rather than holding down an after-school job, they must panhandle or steal to make money in order to eat, and if these methods do not succeed, they often turn to drug dealing or prostitution.

Every day, teen runaways are concerned for their physical safety and must develop methods to protect themselves from violent assaults such as rape. When they do find themselves wounded or sick, their health care options are often extremely limited. Since life on the streets involves hardships that the average teenager never has to face, why do so many teens choose to run away from home each year?

There is no easy answer to this question. Teens leave home for a wide variety of reasons, including trouble in school, arguments with their family, or problems that arise due to their sexual orientation. According to Laurie Schaffner, author of *Teenage Runaways: Broken Hearts and "Bad Attitudes,"* runaways "may leave on impulse, protesting a family quarrel over a rule or an isolated incident."[1] But the main motivation for running away seems to be neglect or abuse at home. They decide that their only chance to survive is to run away, but what many of these teens learn is that they are no safer on the streets than they were with their parents or guardians. The dangers they face are often more harrowing than anything they would face at home; yet when they weigh their options, many of these

Although a life on the streets involves tremendous hardships, many teen runaways view leaving home as their only chance for survival.

Teen runaways rarely seek the help of care facilities or counseling programs. Most contend with the difficulties of runaway life on their own.

teens often choose to stick it out on their own—believing they have at least some control over their lives—rather than return to an environment where they know they will be abused.

Many teens begin their lives on the run with the mistaken assumption that they are embarking on an exciting adventure. Once they hit the streets, however, they quickly discover that their lives are neither glamorous nor thrilling. Though they may meet many new and diverse individuals who seem to be trustworthy, these people are often interested in manipulating them into dealing drugs or entering into activities such as prostitution, pornography, or substance abuse. Runaways rarely find the freedom they seek. More often than not, they find themselves trapped in dangerous circumstances beyond their control.

Hope for help

Helping teen runaways get off the street is a difficult task once they become immersed in a self-destructive lifestyle, but it can be done. For example, Larkin Street Youth Services, located in San Francisco, devotes itself to providing support to teens who consider leaving the streets to become productive members of society. One of the center's major challenges is the fact that runaways often do not want its help. The workers at Larkin Street cannot force anyone to take advantage of their services. All they can do is be available for those who are ready to change their lives.

Though agencies such as Larkin Street are invaluable resources, many people believe that the most important thing is to keep kids from running away in the first place. Education and communication are the main keys to preventing teens from running away. Organizations exist that not only teach teens about the dangers of living on the streets but also are willing to intervene in the home and help families work out their problems together. These approaches are not always successful, but many kids do change their minds about running away once they realize there are alternatives such as family counseling and foster care. Again, however, teens and their families must be willing to take the first step and seek the help they need. Family members, for example, must recognize their problems and begin to work toward correcting them by educating themselves and opening up lines of communication. Once they accept the support and encouragement they need to build healthy relationships, they are less likely to lose their teen to the streets.

1

Who Are Teen Runaways and Why Do They Run?

RUNAWAYS ARE CHILDREN or teenagers who leave home for at least one night without their parents' permission. Statistics show that, in the United States, approximately one in seven kids between the ages of ten and eighteen will run away from home, but determining exactly how many runaways there are is a difficult task. Though no exact numbers are known, social service organizations estimate about 1 million youths currently live on the streets. Approximately 2.8 million adolescents have reported running away at some point in their lives. Some runaways return home after a few days, while others stay on the run for several weeks or months, or never return at all.

According to the National Runaway Switchboard (NRS), there is no typical teen runaway, and no single reason why a runaway leaves home. Runaways are both male and female, although girls more commonly call hotlines for help and are more likely to be arrested. Runaways represent every race and religion, and come from both affluent and poor families. Author Laurie Schaffner says, "There is a common misconception that children from poor families run away more often, that the tensions in working-class families are somehow emotionally and psychologically worse than the problems of middle class

Teen Runaways
Statistics of National Runaway Switchboard Callers

Gender of Caller

Male	24.5%
Female	75.5%

Reported Age of Caller

10	1.0%
11	0.6%
12	1.5%
13	4.0%
14	8.1%
15	14.1%
16	21.6%
17	25.1%
18	9.4%
19	6.5%
20*	3.5%
21*	1.4%
Unknown	3.2%

*started tracking 10/01/2001

Amount of Time Spent on the Street at Time of Call

1–3 Days	42.6%
4–7 Days	21.7%
1–4 Weeks	15.4%
1–2 Months	10.5%
2–6 Months	4.5%
Over 6 Months	5.3%

Problems Cited by Callers

Family Dynamics	41.4%
Peers/Social	14.1%
Youth Services	8.5%
School/Education	7.1%
Mental Health	6.1%
Alcohol/Drug Use	3.9%
Physical Abuse	3.6%
Emotional/Verbal Abuse	3.0%
Economics	2.4%
Transportation	2.2%
Judicial System	2.1%
Neglect	1.6%
Health	1.5%
Gay/Lesbian/Transgendered/Questioning	1.4%
Sexual Abuse/Assault	1.1%

Means of Survival on the Street

Friends/Relatives	47.0%
Unknown	30.5%
Personal Funds	6.7%
Shelters/Soup Kitchens	6.5%
Panhandling	2.3%
Detention/Police	1.8%
Prostitution/Sex Industry	1.7%
Stealing	1.6%
P/T Employment	0.9%
Selling Drugs	0.7%
F/T Employment	0.3%

Source: National Runaway Switchboard.

families, or that working poor people cannot control their children."[2] In reality, runaways do not come solely from lower-income families but from a variety of types of families, and for as many reasons.

While the reasons teens run away are plentiful, about 41 percent cite family dynamics as their main reason for leaving. Teens also run away because of peer pressure or troubles at school. Some are driven by problems with alcohol and drugs, while some are seeking escape from emotionally or verbally abusive living situations. Still others leave because they feel neglected and seek to stir up attention by fleeing. Mental health can sometimes figure in to a teen's decision to leave home, and many kids living on the streets suffer from some sort of mental disorder. Issues relating to sexuality can also cause teens to run because gay, lesbian, and transgender teenagers often feel like they do not belong anywhere, even at home.

No matter what their backgrounds or reasons for leaving are, all teen runaways share a desire to escape their situation and believe that running away is the best way to do so. The fact that many teen runaways would prefer to live on the streets is a testament to how unsafe they feel at home.

Why they run: abusive homes

While problems such as poverty and substance abuse can be among the factors that drive kids to run away, an abusive home environment appears to be the most common motive. Children who grow up in a home where they are subjected to physical violence, sexual abuse, verbal harassment, or emotional manipulation often crave escape. Such experiences are the impetus for a teen to run away, sometimes from situations that are so dire that the dangers of the streets are not recognized by the teen who simply wants out. Author Peter Slavin writes,

> According to two 1997 studies conducted for the U.S. Department of Health and Human Services (HHS), 46% of runaway and homeless youth reported being physically abused, 17% reported being sexually exploited, and 38% reported being emotionally abused. In a survey published by the National Association of Social Workers (NASW), 66% of runaway and homeless youth reported having an alcoholic parent, and 25% reported having a parent who abused drugs.[3]

Mistreatment at the hands of their parents or guardians causes many teens to leave home and try to make it on their own.

In her autobiographical narrative, "I Am a Runaway," posted on *Runaway Lives*, a section of the Penn State–

Lehigh Valley website, an anonymous female discusses her home life and her reasons for leaving. She writes that her father would pick fights with her. These arguments would inevitably escalate into physical altercations after which her father would call the police and have her arrested. Her mother was unwilling to defend her. The girl writes, "My mom was around but the only thing she was good for was to be [my father's] witness. She has this fear that when me and my older sister get older the only person she will have is my dad so she feels she must do anything to protect him. My father has been arrested many times for aggravated child abuse."[4]

Suffering such abuse at home and feeling unprotected is a common cause for flight among runaways. When or if child welfare authorities become aware that a child is living under such conditions, that child may be moved into a foster home. A foster home is supposed to be a safe environment for children whose parents are unable or unwilling to care for them adequately. Though foster care often provides excellent services to kids in need, abuse can occur in these homes as well. It is unclear why some foster homes are sites of abuse. Potential foster parents must go through a rigorous training and screening process before being allowed to care for a child, but this process does not always detect those people who may abuse the children in their care. A report commissioned by the Reagan administration in the late 1980s concluded the following: "Foster care is intended to protect children from neglect and abuse at the hands of parents and other family members, yet all too often it becomes an equally cruel form of neglect and abuse by the state."[5] The problems of the foster care system cause many teenagers to be caught in a destructive cycle: They are placed in a foster home to escape the abuse they receive at home; but finding themselves abused in this new environment, they run away once more. Author Jeffrey Artenstein notes that one female runaway he spoke with at a shelter stated she "had been abused in over ten different foster homes."[6] For a teen such as this girl, no home seems safe.

Suffering emotional and physical abuse leads many teens to leave their homes each year.

Push-outs and throwaways

In many cases, children living in abusive homes are not placed by agencies in alternative living environments. Instead, many young people are either encouraged to leave by their parent or guardian or their decision to leave is met with no opposition from the adults in their lives. They are simply unwanted. These runaways are referred to as "push-outs" or "throwaways."

One young woman using the pen name BabyJill posted her story on the *Runaway Lives* website, where she states that her parents kicked her out of the house for throwing a party when they were not home. When she moved out,

BabyJill did not realize that the situation would be permanent. She ended up moving around quite a bit. She writes, "I stayed with friends mostly for awhile, and then friends of friends, and then friends-of-brother's-uncle's-secretary's-friends and suddenly I realized I was totally lost and a lot of bad things were happening to me at those places where I was staying, so I took it to the streets."[7] Like many throwaways, BabyJill was unable to find a safe place to call home, so she opted to try to make it on her own.

Another youth shares similar circumstances. In his story posted on the same website, he writes that he ran away from home about seven times between the ages of fifteen and seventeen. He claims he was forced to leave home by his parents. Of this experience, he writes, "They sent me to live with an aunt and uncle of mine in another city. They beat their kids, and I was like, I'm either turning you in for that or I'm leaving. They let me leave."[8] His parents allowed him to try living at home once again, but he was disheartened when his mother refused to believe how abusive his aunt and uncle were to his cousins. He felt unable to make things work at home and eventually ran away again.

Gay and lesbian teens are the most vulnerable to being pushed out of their homes. Though support systems do exist for them, many of these teenagers often feel alienated and confused. Their parents may not understand or accept them for who they are; or their friends at school may tease, threaten, or physically harm them because they are perceived as different. Two out of five of these youths have been assaulted, with approximately three-fifths of these incidents occurring in their own homes. Though any teen could be a potential runaway, gay and lesbian teens are particularly at risk. The NRS reports that "sexual minority youth (gay, lesbian, bisexual, trans-gendered, and questioning) are especially vulnerable [to running away]."[9]

An unwanted responsibility

Most families who force their kids to leave are no longer interested in raising their children. The parents of throwaways do not want to deal with the challenges involved in caring for their child. They may be unwilling to accept their child's sexual orientation, or they may simply feel unable to control their child's behavior. Some parents who are financially disadvantaged may no longer feel able to raise their kids. They believe they cannot afford to provide their children with food and shelter, so they want them to leave and fend for themselves. According to Lois Lee, executive director of Children of the Night (an organization based in Van Nuys, California), "Often we call a girl's home and her parents will say, 'No, she can't come back.' Sometimes we even get calls from parents who want us to take their children from them."[10] Situations such as these only add to the growing number of children and teens who are living on the streets.

Some parents actually abandon their children, who are left to fend for themselves indefinitely, sometimes in a new, unfamiliar location. Luree Nicholson of L.A. Youth Network reports one teen's story of abandonment: "We stopped at a gas station and I went to the bathroom. When I came out, they were gone."[11] This type of situation often results in the teen turning to the streets for survival, since he or she no longer has a family to depend on, even for minimal support. For teens who are abandoned by their parents, as well as those who are throwaways or push-outs, the future looks grim. With no love or support from their families, they often come to believe that living alone on the streets is the only answer.

An unhealthy environment

Another reason teens leave home is the presence of alcohol or drug abuse in the home. One in four children lives in a home with an alcoholic, and many others live with parents or other relatives who abuse drugs. When under the influence of these substances, parents may be unable to function adequately enough to perform everyday tasks for their children, such as cooking meals, driving to school, keeping a clean house, and providing clothes and other necessities. Living in a clean and safe environment is compromised when a caretaker's primary concern is feeding an addiction, not raising his or her children.

Some parents abandon their teens altogether. These teens often believe that a life on the streets is their only option.

In his research on runaways and homeless teens, Jeffrey Artenstein discovered how difficult the home life of children whose parents abuse drugs can be. Artenstein writes, "Common is the home where one or both parents are drug addicts for whom the child's welfare is secondary to the next fix." Parents under the influence may not be aware when a child is hurt or ill and in need of medical attention. Addicted parents may not be able to give their children *any* attention, leaving teens feeling insecure, isolated, and neglected. Since drugs and alcohol can make it difficult for a person to think clearly, parents who abuse these substances

Alcohol and drug abuse by a parent or guardian is cited by many teens as their primary reason for running away.

may not be able to discern how poorly they are caring for their families. "Some of these parents," writes Artenstein, "[even] incorporate their child into their schemes to score drugs."[12] Under such circumstances, many teens face serious health and safety risks on a daily basis. Though these parents may not physically harm their children, they are regularly putting these teens in a dangerous position by exposing them to drugs and drug dealers.

Other reasons teens run away

Not all kids who leave home are pushed out, nor do they necessarily leave due to abuse or neglect. Some teens run away for more minor reasons such as the desire to follow a friend who has already run away. Some leave because they fear fallout from a poor test grade or a bad report card. Others may run because they have experienced an argument or misunderstanding at home.

When these events occur, some teens may feel trapped. While most adults have developed the skills necessary to deal with problems as they arise, many teens have not. They may feel extraordinarily confused, scared, or overwhelmed

Neglected teens will sometimes run away to gain the attention of their parents.

by what feel like large problems. Running away, therefore, can be a teen's attempt at either solving or escaping their problems.

Teens may also run away to get attention. For neglected teens who grow up in households where they feel overlooked or pushed aside, sometimes running away becomes a means to grab their parents' or other authority figures' attention. Artenstein refers to these kids as "unlikely runaways" and says they "run away following a minor family argument, or simply for adventure."[13] When teens leave under these circumstances, they usually return home within a few days and rarely end up making a habit of running away. Regardless of their reasons for leaving, these kids are still putting themselves in danger by trying to live on their own.

The hazards teen runaways face on the streets every day are extreme. Learning what these dangers are is essential to understanding just how desperate these teens feel. They are willing to put their very lives in jeopardy in order to avoid returning to a home life that they see as far more problematic. Though life on the street *is* more often than not more perilous than their home life, many of these teens convince themselves that they are better off on their own.

2

Life on the Streets

FOR MANY KIDS, running away seems like an exciting adventure, and the first few days on their own may be fun. They meet new people, have new experiences, and enjoy their independence. But after the novelty wears off, these kids realize that street life is hazardous. Some are able to escape this world, either by returning home or by seeking help at a shelter. Others, however, get drawn into the lifestyle of a homeless youth and have to learn to fend for themselves against the dangers of living on the street. As BabyJill, one runaway, puts it, "You think you're running from the pain, but you're really just diving headfirst into the worst pain of your life."[14]

Surviving homelessness

Unlike most other teens, runaways usually do not receive any practical or emotional support from their families. They are often young and unprepared to handle the responsibilities of setting up and maintaining a home on their own. As a result, many runaways end up homeless, and they are forced to develop methods for survival.

Many teens run to big cities such as New York and Los Angeles. These cities are magnets for runaways from all over the country; in San Francisco, for example, only 8 percent of the approximately two thousand runaways on the street per night are from the area. Most are looking for a place where there are other runaways, and where they believe they can blend in and go unnoticed by the authorities. Large cities also offer a wide range of services for homeless

Homeless teens encounter many dangers on city streets, including violent crime and sexual abuse.

and runaway youth, including temporary shelters that provide food and clothing. These services are a big attraction for runaways concerned with the possibility of needing help once they are on their own.

Large cities rarely end up being the havens runaways think them to be, and kids find themselves struggling to simply find a safe place to sleep. Abandoned buildings—or "squats," as they are referred to on the streets—often become home for these kids. Squats often house dozens of homeless people at a time, attracting both young and old. Though runaways feel safer in these buildings than they do on the streets, drug abuse and dangerous sexual encounters often occur in such environments. In some cities, police routinely check abandoned buildings to make sure no one is living in them. When this happens, runaways are forced to move on to another squat or to find somewhere else to live. They may seek shelter under freeway overpasses or in junked cars, or they may crowd into a motel room for a night or two when the weather is bad.

Because the night brings various dangers for those living on the streets—beatings and muggings are common occurrences after dark—many runaways become nocturnal, sleeping during the day because it is safer. One homeless boy, Raider, who was interviewed by writer Robert McGarvey, believes that, for the homeless, sleeping during the day is just common sense. He says, "Too much happens at night. If you're asleep, you can get stabbed, robbed."[15]

Some homeless kids attempt to find help and safety at shelters. In many cases, these shelters are true sanctuaries for kids who need to get off the streets. Some shelters, however, are as dangerous as the streets themselves, and the kids who stay there are at risk of being seriously harmed. In fact, according to author Julia Gilden, many teenage runaways "say they are afraid to stay in adult shelters because they are often taken advantage of by older transients [homeless people who move around a lot from town to town or from shelter to shelter]."[16] Teen runaways fear these transients will steal what little money or valuables they own. They are also at risk for violence at the hands of these adults, who could harm them physically or sexually.

Sticking together

One way homeless adolescents attempt to protect themselves is by sticking together. Often traveling in packs of three to fifteen kids, they create mutual protection societies and look out for one another on the streets. In some situations, these groupings can break up as quickly as they are formed, and many runaways are left with no stable relationships or loyalties to other people. In other situations, however, the teens develop lasting friendships on the streets. According to Kevin Jackson, street outreach manager of Our Town Family Center in Tucson, Arizona, the bonds these teenagers develop with each other often resemble actual families. He notes, "A lot of kids who end up living on the streets have found surrogate families out there. In fact, the language of the street even reflects that. They call each other 'street brother' and 'street sister.'"[17] These labels extend to cover a range of familial roles. For example, the adolescents who assume parental roles are often referred to as "street mom" or "street dad." These teens are usually a little older or are simply wiser about street life. They protect inexperienced runaways, helping them to find food and shelter. The kids who have such relationships begin to view these people as their actual family. Even though they do not have a house to live in, they still feel that they have a home.

Networks of friends, however, rarely substitute for a real family. The anonymous girl who wrote "I Am a Runaway" for the *Runaway Lives* website admits that friendships are not always enough when it comes to surviving on the streets. She writes, "I feel so alone even though I have friends who I know care about me. It is just hard to think where is my next meal coming from, where am I going to sleep tonite, or when is the next time I am gonna be able to shower. Everything changes when you are a runaway—everything changes."[18] For runaways who find themselves homeless, even the best friendships cannot replace what they need most, a safe home environment.

"Dumpster diving"

Teen runaways must also figure out how to obtain food and money. Finding food is perhaps their biggest challenge, and many runaways suffer from malnutrition. They often must resort to unconventional methods in order to get something to eat. Raider, for example, goes "trashing" for his food, which, according to Peter Slavin, involves "root[ing] through garbage cans in search of stale bread, over-ripe fruit, peanut butter jars with a few scrapes left, maybe a steak bone with a hunk or two of meat."[19]

Also known as "dumpster diving," trashing is a common practice among runaways and the homeless; but food is not the only thing they search for in garbage bins. In many states, soda and beer cans, as well as bottles, can be redeemed for a few cents apiece. Some runaways dumpster dive in an attempt to find empty, discarded beverage containers which they can return to grocery stores for a little

In some cases, homeless youths will band together to function like a family, developing personal relationships of mutual protection and assistance.

"Dumpster diving," which involves sifting through waste containers for food and recyclables, is a popular means of subsistence among runaways.

extra money. When this method fails to work, many runaways resort to begging.

Begging for money on the streets

Since most homeless kids are poverty-stricken, panhandling—or begging for money on the street—is also a popular way to raise cash. In his article "Runaways: Children of
the Night," Robert McGarvey's conversation with Melodie,
a young runaway, makes clear the lengths homeless kids
will go to in order to raise money. He writes,

> They are . . . penniless and, for cash, Melodie admits to doing
> what most other street kids do. "I get by pan handling. You
> get $5, $10 a day. That's plenty." With the money, she'll
> splurge and buy french fries—always drenched in free
> ketchup—and a soda, possibly a shake. What's left will buy
> cigarettes, to be passed around to the kids in her pack.[20]

In many areas, begging for money is not against the law.
As long as runaways behave politely to the passersby from
whom they wish to collect money, they are usually allowed
to panhandle as much as they need to.

When panhandling is not an option, or when they are unable to raise enough cash in this manner, runaways often
turn to criminal behavior. For many runaways, as McGarvey
notes, "when times toughen, they snatch purses, shoplift and
smash car windows to grab a radio or briefcase."[21]

Drug dealing

Panhandling and stealing are not the only ways that runaways make money; many also turn to dealing drugs.
These runaways are often manipulated into doing so by
older criminals, usually homeless males. These men offer
to protect the youths from violence and other dangers of
street life in exchange for sexual favors and help dealing
drugs. By selling illegal substances, runaways may earn
extra cash or they may simply receive food and shelter
from the adults who have recruited them to commit crimes.

Some runaways get involved in drug dealing on their
own. Though there is the possibility that these teens will
make money in this business, it is more likely that they

will jeopardize their health and safety. Violence against drug-dealing runaways is not uncommon, and their constant exposure to these substances puts them at risk of becoming addicts themselves.

"Survival sex"

Another activity that many runaways rely on to obtain money and other basic needs is "survival sex." Survival sex involves offering sex in exchange for food, money, or a place to stay. Teens who engage in survival sex are not prostitutes, because they resort to this behavior for basic necessities and do not use sex to make a living on a regular basis. In his paper on the health needs of homeless youth, Dr. James A. Farrow cites survival sex as one of the most common ways for runaways to obtain funds. He writes,

> Few young women who are on the streets for any period of time fail to become involved [in survival sex] and, although young males have more options available for survival, they too are likely to become involved in hustling or other forms of "survival" sex. Street youth often exchange sexual activity for food, shelter, drugs, or protection, from someone who is older and more streetwise.[22]

Although those who turn to survival sex are not the same as prostitutes, many homeless runaways do end up getting involved in the business of prostitution because it can be profitable for kids who are desperate.

Prostitution and pornography

Teen runaways are vulnerable to those people who wish to exploit them sexually through pornography and prostitution. In "Girls and the Business of Sex," Andrea D'Asaro writes,

> Approximately one hundred million street children around the world start their days early in the morning, earning a meager income selling candy, shining shoes, picking rags, or engaging in petty crimes. "If they don't earn enough for the day, some know they can always turn a trick," says Marilyn Rocky, Director of ChildHope International in New York.[23]

According to the Paul & Lisa Program for exploited youth, based in Essex, Connecticut, most victims fall

between the ages of thirteen and seventeen, but children as young as ten are actively recruited for prostitution and pornography. In many instances, these kids are forced or otherwise coerced into becoming involved in these activities.

Child pornography is defined by the Paul & Lisa Program as a situation which "involves the coercion of children into sexual activity for the purpose of producing, distributing or possessing print, visual, or electronic media that portrays the minors in sexual activity."[24] Though this business is illegal, it is difficult to protect children from it due to increased access to pornographic materials on the Internet. Pedophiles—adult individuals who are sexually

Begging for change can provide enough money for homeless teens to survive from day to day.

attracted to children—are the primary criminals who exploit minors in this manner. Runaways are especially vulnerable to such exploitation, as they are desperate for both money and acceptance.

Child prostitution involves sexual activity provided by minors to adults in exchange for money and, like child pornography, is considered a serious crime. The Paul & Lisa Program website says the following about this business:

> Children may be forced by their pimp [a man who acts as a prostitute's boss] to prostitute on the street or through escort services. Under the pimp's domineering watch, or even under the control of another prostitute in the pimp's [employment], they may solicit business in dance clubs, hotels, bars, restaurants, and casinos, to name but a few likely locales. Male prostitution is extremely common; most boy prostitutes provide sexual services to other males.[25]

Susan Breault, assistant director of the Paul & Lisa Program for exploited youth, estimates the number of child prostitutes at about 1 million. Statistics show that 49 percent of child prostitutes are girls and 51 percent are boys.

Varee Suthireung is an example of a runaway who turned first to survival sex, and then to prostitution. She began running away at age nine to escape a home where her father sexually abused her. Varee's parents gave up custody of her when she was thirteen; but she ran away from her foster homes and other placement centers, and used sex as a means of survival. In a 1993 interview, Varee

Prostitution appeals to some homeless teens as a fast means of obtaining money.

claims that, at first, she would often trade sexual activity for hamburgers and french fries. By the time she turned fifteen, however, obtaining drugs became more important to her than food. She began prostituting herself to support a drug habit; and from there, her life took a turn for the worse. "After a night of drugs, drinking, and being passed from one man to another, [Varee] tried to kill herself by driving a motorcycle into a brick wall. Miraculously, she survived and moved in with a drug dealer and pimp until, strung out on heroin, she could no longer sell her body."[26] Varee became too sickly to work as a prostitute, and her pimp eventually kicked her out.

Though it is common for prostitutes to be as young as Varee, children even younger than thirteen are drawn into the business, and in some cases are preferred. Some customers of prostitution assume that very young children are free from sexually transmitted diseases and are therefore "safer" than other prostitutes. This is not true, according to author Andrea D'Asaro, who notes that "children are most vulnerable to HIV infection because of easily torn genitals, as well as lack of power or education to insist on safe sex."[27] Varee herself was HIV-positive, and though she was able to turn her life around and leave the streets, she eventually died of AIDS.

Runaways are often easily drawn into prostitution. According to Dr. James A. Farrow, "Many youth have little or no knowledge of prostitution when they first reach the street, but after talking with involved peers who seem to be making easy money, it becomes less frightening."[28] Once they become involved in prostitution it is tough for them to stop. In some cases, their pimps threaten them with physical abuse in order to keep them working. In other cases, the kids continue to prostitute themselves because they need to make money in order to survive on the streets. Gay and lesbian runaways are even more likely than their heterosexual peers to provide sex for money. They are in search of a place where they can feel accepted for who they are, and as a result, they are often easily manipulated by people who intend to exploit them.

"What do you want?"

For a runaway like Timmy, one of the homeless teens interviewed by Robert McGarvey, prostituting himself seems to be a logical option. When asked by potential customers if he is a prostitute, he responds, "What do you want and how much [money] do you got?"[29] Shannon, a runaway in San Francisco, is not as casual as Timmy seems to be when it comes to prostitution. She does, however, believe that her involvement with prostitution proves she can survive independent of her father. She also sees her circumstances as temporary and believes that her father will have to respect her more for learning how to take care of herself. "Things will be different when I go back to Virginia and live with my dad," she says. "Now that he knows I can make it on my own, he won't dare hit me anymore. I have power over him instead of the other way around."[30]

Other runaways, such as Laurie, see prostitution as a last resort, something to do only when she's broke. Laurie says, "I hate whoring. It's scary. You never know about the dudes who pick you up."[31] But as scary as it may be for her, she still turns to sex as a way to make money when no other options are apparent.

A deadly business

The business of prostitution exposes runaways to the possibility of being raped, beaten, or even murdered. Evidence suggests that violence inflicted upon juvenile prostitutes at the hands of their pimps or customers has increased. The Paul & Lisa Program cites black eyes, visible scarring, broken bones, and extensive bruising as proof of brutality against young prostitutes. According to their website, "[Such violence] is physically and psychologically harmful and is also used as a means of degradation intended to erode individualism and self-esteem."[32] Violence against runaways traps them in a depressing cycle: The worse an adolescent's self-confidence is, the more likely he or she will continue working as a prostitute. The adults they become involved with in this business often use their physical strength to assert power and control over the young prostitutes.

Young homeless men and women are typically driven to prostitution only out of extreme desperation.

Prostitution exposes runaways to the possibility of being beaten, raped, or even murdered.

The experience of Becca Hedman is a prime example of the danger of violence on the streets. A thirteen-year-old runaway who worked the streets as a prostitute, Becca met a violent death. Her father, Dennis Hedman, describes the crime:

> She's standing on a street corner. She gets picked up by a 36-year-old white male who pays her $50 to have sex. She accompanies him back to his room, they perform the act. He was not satisfied, wanted his money back. Uh, Becca told him no. She turned her back to get dressed. He pulled a baseball bat from—out from under the bed and beat her to death.[33]

Though Becca's story seems extreme, it is not unusual. Many teen runaways, particularly those involved with drugs or prostitution, end up dead as a result of violent assault. This is not the only hazard teen runaways face. Those involved with prostitution run the risk of contracting sexually transmitted diseases and AIDS, and runaways in general are forced to cope with a wide variety of health problems as they attempt to survive life on the streets.

3

Runaways Face Serious Health Risks

HOMELESS RUNAWAYS ARE at particularly high risk for a wide variety of serious health problems. They face exposure to sexually transmitted diseases (STDs), malnutrition, pregnancy, suicide, and homicide. Because these adolescents live in dangerous environments, and because their lifestyles often include activities such as alcohol and drug abuse and unprotected survival sex or prostitution, they are more likely to be forced to cope with dangerous illnesses and other problematic health concerns than nonhomeless teens. Runaways also must deal with mental health problems such as depression and behavioral disorders.

Trish Crawford, a reporter who interviewed runaways on the streets of Toronto, Canada, describes Melissa, a homeless girl with serious health problems. Crawford writes, "[Melissa] doesn't brush [her teeth] after meals, her skin is breaking out and she is fighting a bladder infection that isn't getting any better because she keeps losing her medication, along with her gloves and nearly everything else she owns."[34] Sometimes Melissa sleeps in a shelter, but she has no problem sleeping outside if necessary, huddling with her friends in a money-machine kiosk. Despite her survival instincts, Melissa's vagrant lifestyle contributes to her poor health. Ruth Ewert, a woman who runs a health clinic in Toronto states that a large percentage of the youths who come to her clinic suffer from illnesses that, under other conditions, are easily treatable. These commonly include skin infections and upper respiratory problems, which are caused mainly by poor nutrition and crowded and unsanitary living conditions.

HIV

One of the most prevalent, and most deadly, health risks on the streets is HIV, the virus that causes AIDS. Runaways are ten times more likely than their peers to develop HIV. Though many people contract AIDS through intravenous drug use, most homeless youths become infected

Homeless runaways are at higher risk for serious illnesses, which may go untreated for extended periods of time.

with the disease through unprotected sex. Ruth Ewert has tried to educate runaways about safe sex, encouraging them to use condoms whenever they engage in sexual activity. But Ewert's efforts are often fruitless. She says, "Many say they don't expect to be alive five years from now, so why bother?"[35]

Jerry, a former runaway who spent time on the streets of San Francisco, is HIV-positive. He was thrown out of his home in the tenth grade and went to San Francisco in the hopes of finding people who would accept his homosexuality. He quickly became addicted to intravenous drugs and worked the streets as a male prostitute. When he found out he had HIV at the age of nineteen, he realized the mistakes he had made in his life. "I guess I never really wanted to die," he said. "I just grew up a bit and realized I really wanted to live."[36] With hard work and help from social services, Jerry was able to turn his life around. Though he still suffers from the disease, he was able to go to school and get a good job.

Pregnancy

While unprotected sex puts many teenage runaways at risk for contracting sexually transmitted diseases, it can also lead to unwanted pregnancy. One in five girls living on the streets will get pregnant, and for them, pregnancy has its own health risks. Many of these mothers-to-be are unable to find adequate health care and are therefore unable to protect themselves and their babies from possible complications during their pregnancies. Pregnancy is dangerous enough for young mothers: Those under the age of seventeen are even more likely than women in their twenties to develop pregnancy-related problems. Lack of proper health care, however, only increases the risks that a pregnant teen may face. For example, if left untreated, pregnancy-induced hypertension (high blood pressure brought on by pregnancy) can cause the mother to suffer heart failure or a stroke and can result in the death of both mother and child. It is therefore very dangerous for pregnant teens to be out on the streets without proper prenatal care.

Pregnant runaways are often unable to give their unborn children necessary prenatal care. Many of these runaways do not eat balanced meals on a regular basis, and are therefore not providing their babies with the food and vitamins they need for development in the womb. The unsanitary and dangerous living conditions common to many runaways put both mother and child at risk for a variety of dangerous infections. The abuse of alcohol, cigarettes, and drugs that many runaways engage in is also terribly dangerous to a fetus. Many homeless teens have low-birth-weight babies, who will be at risk for many health problems, and may not survive at all.

Alcohol abuse

Over-consumption of alcohol is rampant among homeless runaways. It is the substance they most frequently abuse. Approximately 60 to 80 percent of homeless and runaway youth drink alcohol regularly, and about one-fifth of them drink to intoxication at least once a week. Heather, a teen runaway interviewed by Julia Gilden for her article "See How They Run," gets drunk on wine. She says, "I drink because I'm scared. I'm scared all the time."[37] Even though runaways such as Heather are underage, alcohol is easy for them to obtain. Many runaways resort to stealing the alcohol they want or rely on their older friends to purchase it for them.

Runaways can suffer many health problems stemming from alcohol abuse. Frequent and heavy use of alcohol, for example, can lead to liver damage. Alcohol poisoning is another potentially dangerous outcome of abusing alcohol. Such poisoning often requires medical attention and can be fatal if health care is not forthcoming, a situation common to homeless runaways.

The very lifestyle associated with alcohol and drug use can be hazardous for runaways. While "under the influence," their judgment is impaired and they are more likely to have accidents or suffer injury. When they are drunk or high, they may make unwise decisions regarding their physical safety. They may carelessly have unprotected sex,

Alcoholism is rampant among homeless teens, with the vast majority drinking to the point of intoxication at least once a week.

which puts them at greater risk for contracting STDs and becoming pregnant. The fact that they are homeless makes these already serious problems dangerous.

Drug abuse

In addition to abusing alcohol, many runaways use dangerous drugs because they are easy to obtain on the streets. According to a counselor at the Larkin Street Youth Services "There is no way to live on the streets and not be involved in drugs."[38] Studies funded by the National Institute on Drug

Abuse (NIDA) report that homeless and runaway youths are more at risk for abusing drugs than teens who live at home. Marijuana, cocaine, crack, ecstasy, and heroin are among the substances most commonly used by runaways.

While drug use and drug dealing, as well as other activities involving illegal goods, are harmful in themselves, the lifestyle associated with these can put the runaway in further jeopardy. Since many people—teens and adults alike—who live on the streets rely on drugs and alcohol for their survival, many will resort to violence in order to protect the drugs they need to get through the day. A runaway who enters this world is at risk of becoming a victim of its violence.

Drug abuse also makes runaways, both male and female, more vulnerable to rape. Janet, a young runaway from Toronto, was raped while sleeping outdoors. According to writer Trish Crawford, Janet had "broken Rule Number One: never be alone. She was so stoned at the time she doesn't quite remember what happened but did not report it to the police. 'I couldn't tell the cops. We're always being hassled by the cops.'"[39] In Janet's case, and in the case of many other runaways like her, drug use not only made her more vulnerable to violence, but it also made it impossible for her to remember the details of the attack—important information she could have passed on to the authorities.

Though illegal substances may help runaways survive emotionally for a short time, substance abuse can eventually make it difficult for them to cope in their everyday lives. In a situation where their lives are already unstable, drugs and alcohol can make matters worse by leading many young runaways to commit suicide. One NIDA-sponsored study, which involved 640 youths staying in shelters and 600 teens living on the streets, found that approximately "25 percent of the shelter youths and nearly one-third of the street youths had tried to kill themselves at least once in their lives. In both groups, those who had abused drugs—especially sedatives, hallucinogens, and inhalants—were far more likely than nonusers to have attempted suicide."[40]

Involvement with drugs can make it all the more difficult for runaways to seek help from community services when they are considering suicide.

Psychological disorders

The negative effects of living on the street are most visible in the scars and bruises caused by violent activity and in the obvious ill health of many young runaways. Psychological problems, though often less apparent than physical problems, can be equally harmful to those who must endure them. According to Dr. James A. Farrow, homeless youth are more likely than their nonhomeless peers to "suffer from a wide range of mental health problems, which often coexist with physical and substance abuse problems."[41] Among runaways there exist high rates of various types of depression, other psychological disorders, and suicide attempts.

It is difficult to be sure if runaways are suffering from depression prior to leaving home or if their psychological disorders are a result of street life. Sociologists at the University of Nebraska–Lincoln, involved in a three-year study of homeless youth, are trying to figure this out. Of the runaways interviewed for this study, 42 percent have indicated that they suffer from depression or conduct disorder, a serious behavioral problem defined by psychiatrist Michael G. Connor as "a persistent pattern in which the basic rights of others and important social norms and rules are violated."[42] Behaviors associated with this disorder include stealing, lying, arson and other types of vandalism to property, and physical violence against other people or animals. When runaways suffering from a conduct disorder engage in these types of behaviors, they are not doing so merely to be rebellious; these teens find it difficult, if not impossible, to control their actions. According to the University of Nebraska–Lincoln study, 74 percent of males and 57 percent of females living on the street have a conduct disorder.

The high rate of suicide attempts among runaways is one of the main reasons that their mental health problems need to be addressed. One of the major causes of death for teenagers living on the streets is suicide, an act frequently brought on due to depression or other types of psychological ailments. According to James A. Farrow, many runaways are actively suicidal, which means they have made repeated attempts at taking their own lives. Other runaways may try to kill themselves once but make no other attempts. In a 1992 study of homeless youth, Farrow and his colleagues found that

The psychological and emotional scars of street life drive many homeless teens to attempt suicide.

Lifetime suicide attempts were reported by 24% of runaways in New York City shelters and by 18% of runaways using an

outpatient clinic in Los Angeles. About half of another Hollywood "street" sample had attempted suicide sometime in their lives. Of those who had made an attempt, more than half had attempted more than once, and more than half had attempted suicide in the previous 12 months.[43]

In both cities, the researchers discovered that females are more likely than males to try to kill themselves. They also learned that about two-thirds of homeless kids who are hospitalized for depression or other mental health concerns are admitted after attempting suicide.

In many cases, young runaways are unaware that they are suffering from serious psychological disorders; they do not spend time with people who are qualified to recognize their symptoms. As a result, these teens do not seek the medical attention they need in order to become emotionally healthy.

Obstacles to obtaining health care

Health and social service organizations do exist to give runaways at least some of the help that they need. Still, there are many obstacles to obtaining comprehensive health care for a person living on the street. Farrow and his colleagues cite a number of barriers that runaways face when they seek medical attention. When runaways seek assistance at a hospital emergency room, for example, "they are likely to be asked for a permanent address, health insurance information, and parental permission for treatment."[44] Many runaways do not have health insurance, and if they do, it is paid for by their parents, which means the hospital or clinic workers would be obligated to contact their families. Also, health care providers who work in emergency rooms must have parental consent to treat people under the age of eighteen. Since many of these teens leave home because of abuse or neglect, contacting their parents before receiving medical attention is not an option for them. They want the services they receive to remain confidential because they do not wish to be reconciled with their families. In some cases, the adults in their lives have exploited and victimized them to such an extent that

they no longer trust anyone, including the health care professionals who wish to help them. When faced with the
possibility of being reunited with their parents or guardians
against their wishes, runaways are unlikely to seek medical aid.

Other problems exist for homeless youth when seeking
health care. Underage runaways or those with police
records fear their visit to the doctor will lead to the notification of police or a social service agency. Health care is
also expensive, and many of these teens cannot afford a
visit to the doctor or the medicine necessary to get better.
In many cases, they will choose to ignore an obvious need
for medical attention. If they seek aid at all, it is often long
after an illness has progressed, when it is sometimes too
late for medical professionals to help them. And because
these kids often move around from place to place, rarely
staying in one location for very long, they are unable to
seek follow-up care from their medical provider.

Finding health care on the streets

Health and social service organizations are trying to
help teen runaways. Though health care services specifically designed for the homeless are not as comprehensive
as the providers would like them to be, many outreach
programs do exist. Some cities, such as Seattle, Washington, for example, provide free street-side medical assistance to youth in need. This program, set up by the
Division of Adolescent Medicine at the University of
Washington in partnership with youth outreach programs,
has been very successful. Not only has it helped to elimi-
nate the many obstacles runaways face when seeking
medical attention, but it also helps to make local physi-
cians aware of the problem of runaways' health care.
These types of programs are capable of diagnosing and
treating a variety of illnesses, including the common cold
and STDs. Some even offer HIV testing. New York,
Boston, San Francisco, and Los Angeles, along with many
other urban areas, have similar street-side and mobile
health service programs in place.

Although programs exist to provide medical assistance to homeless youths, many runaways suffer from a variety of untreated illnesses.

Larkin Street Youth Services in San Francisco began testing homeless youths for the AIDS virus in 1991. From the program's conception to 1997, staffers noticed a large increase in the number of youth testing positive for the disease. In response to this crisis, they opened the Assisted Care and After Care Facility on Hyde Street to help young people infected with HIV. This program, funded in large part by taxpayers, seems to be working, as shown by the large number of teen runaways taking advantage of its services.

Though fighting AIDS and other illnesses among runaways is a difficult task, many programs are still willing to put forth the effort to offer hope for sick teens living on their own. These programs may be helpful for runaways who are ill, but they cannot help those teens who face other sorts of obstacles, such as trouble with the law.

4

Runaways and the Law

IN SOME STATES, when a teenager runs away from home, he or she is subject to possible arrest and detainment. For a teen under arrest, a juvenile detention center is generally used instead of an adult facility, such as a prison. Being detained is not the same as being arrested. Detention can mean waiting with a law enforcement official while the runaway's parents are contacted and arrangements are made for returning the teen home. It can also involve being taken to the police station and held there for hours or even for days as the authorities decide how to best handle the situation. According to author R. Barri Flowers,

> A runaway's contact with police occurs primarily through arrest, detention, and returning the runaway home or placing them in a juvenile facility. The nature of this contact is based on a number of factors including reports of missing youth, the type of runaway episode, police department size, and varying laws with respect to dealing with runaway children.[45]

While many states do not treat the problem of running away as an offense worthy of arrest or detainment, other states have stricter rules governing runaways and often place these teens in juvenile detention centers. Although runaways can also be arrested for partaking in more serious criminal acts such as drug dealing or prostitution, often they are arrested simply because of their status as runaways.

Once a teen is considered an adult, leaving home without a parent's permission is not considered a legal problem. Paul Ludwig, founder and CEO of Teen Rescue in Corona,

California, says that "each state and/or county has their own laws [regarding running away and the legal age for teens to live on their own]. In California a teenager becomes an adult at the age of 18. Many states [say] the child is an adult at the age of 17. In Canada, it's 16."[46] When a teen leaves home prior to becoming a legal adult in his or her state, it creates the possibility of legal involvement.

Not only do the laws regarding runaways differ from state to state, but the rights of parents, law enforcement

In certain states, homeless teens are arrested solely on the basis of their status as runaways.

and other government agencies, and those who intend to help these teens also vary by state. Some states allow parents to request that their child be found and arrested, while other states insist that illegal behavior must occur before police can take runaways into custody. Other states automatically treat runaways as criminals, particularly if they run away from a foster home. In these cases, the teens are arrested and often returned to the homes from which they fled. Whatever the circumstances, once the law gets involved in the life of a runaway, that teen will have to face the legal consequences of running away from home.

The basic rights of runaways and their parents

Even though the laws regarding runaways vary depending on which state the runaway is in, these teens and their parents still have rights that remain consistent no matter where they live. Writer Lillian Ambrosino points out, for example, that teenagers have the right to minimal standards of living and to live in a safe home environment. Even if their home is not a loving atmosphere, they have the right to know that their safety will not be threatened. These needs are not always met, which is why many teenagers choose to leave home in the first place.

But just as teenagers have rights, so too do their parents. As Ambrosino puts it, parents "have a right to know where their child is; to expect that while he is still dependent on them for a livelihood he will obey their just and reasonable demands."[47] Parents who set sensible rules for their children, such as giving them curfews and asking them to do chores around the house, have the right to expect that their children will follow these guidelines.

Not all parents of runaways are cruel and abusive toward their children, however, and not all runaways are mere victims of their circumstances. In some instances, teens who end up running away are very difficult to live with, and their parents are making honest efforts to make things work out in the home. Some areas of the country do not have adequate laws for handling runaway cases, but the laws that do exist—even if they are not always appropriate for every youth—are in place in an effort to protect both runaways and their parents.

When running away is illegal

Some states classify teen runaways as criminals. They can be considered criminals even if they have not been found to be guilty of other illegal activities or behaviors. The major motivation to arrest or detain young runaways is to find them on their parents' behalf. In states where runaways are considered criminals, police departments and other agencies often have authority to treat them as juvenile delinquents. "Juvenile delinquent" is a term usually applied to a person under the age of eighteen who is guilty of criminal behaviors, defined by the particular state and its laws. Delinquent acts can include the same kinds of crimes that adults are found guilty of, but they can also include such acts as running away from home. In states where runaways are considered to be juvenile delinquents, police may choose to either send these teens home or to a juvenile detention facility.

Juvenile detention facilities hold young people who have been found guilty of illegal activity. The youths who live in detention halls are usually between the ages of eleven and seventeen. They are forced to follow rules, which include having limited visitors and telephone calls, and they are not allowed to leave the premises until they are officially released, unless they receive permission to leave temporarily for a special circumstance such as a death in the family. The rules in a detention hall are strictly enforced but may be relaxed for those juveniles who display good behavior.

Life in a detention center is not unlike life in an adult prison. Many facilities place the juveniles in cells, which are often very small and have only one window, if any. A cell may include a toilet and a sink, which means the juveniles have much less privacy than they would were they allowed to use a regular bathroom. The young inmates are not allowed to have many personal possessions in their

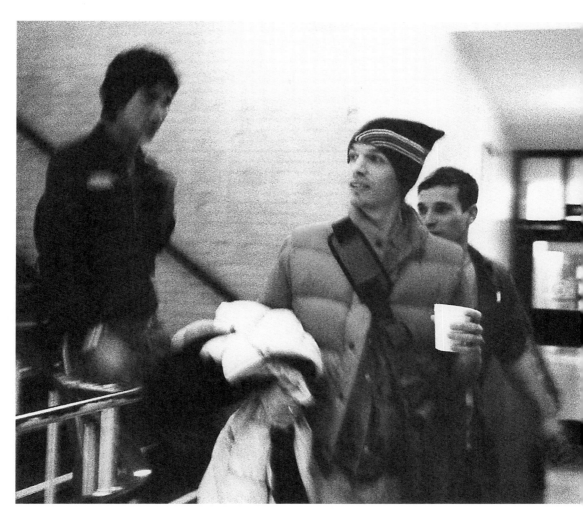

cells; even their clothing and bedding is provided by the staff. Meals are usually served in a cafeteria setting.

Many of these facilities offer important services, like continuing education programs. Though they may be away from their normal school environment, these teens are still expected to study and earn an education. In some cases, the school will deliver assignments to the youths in the facility. When this is not possible, the juvenile center has teachers on staff who will design coursework for the teens.

The facilities also offer medical care for all of the residents. Some detention centers even allow parents to pick

Some states treat minors who run away as juvenile delinquents, giving authorities the power to detain them.

their child up for doctor's appointments if that child has a serious health problem. The teens are often allowed to participate in indoor and outdoor recreational activities as well as arts and crafts. Discussion groups and counseling sessions may also be held, which cover topics such as anger management and drug and alcohol education. Though a juvenile detention hall may not be the ideal environment for every teen, many of these facilities are dedicated to helping young offenders reform.

When juvenile detention facilities are not available, however, it can be detrimental to classify runaways as criminals. For example, if they are arrested in small towns that do not have separate facilities for young offenders, police officers are forced to place runaways in adult prisons. Since runaways are young and rarely guilty of violent crimes such as murder, placing them in prisons with hardened criminals can negatively influence them and actually put them at risk for committing more serious crimes.

When running away is not illegal

Many states do not use arrest or detainment when dealing with teen runaways. In these states, runaways are classified as status offenders, which means they are under the age of eighteen. They are not classified as criminal offenders. These teens are usually not sent to reformatories or other detention facilities. They are either returned home or, if the home is deemed unsafe due to abuse or neglect, brought to a shelter. Other times they are referred to a social service agency.

The Children's Aid Society in West Texas, for example, is an agency that runs a teen shelter and offers an alternative to detention for runaway youths. According to Amy Burgess, a reporter for the *Times Record News*, "The society has an arrangement with juvenile probation and law-enforcement officers to allow runaways to be taken to the shelter instead of to juvenile detention."[48] Since detention halls can often be sites of violence, the shelter is a less threatening environment for runaway teens, many of whom have been abused at home or by members of their foster family. Use of the shelter also helps reduce overpopulation in detention facilities and makes it easier to serve the families of runaways. Whenever possible, the aid society's ultimate goal is to reunite these young people with their loved ones, as long as their home environment is safe.

Other states have no set standards for how to deal with these troubled teens, and their laws are more lenient than the parents and caretakers of runaways would like them to be. For example, in Pennsylvania, the law prohibits arresting or detaining teen runaways, regardless of the parents' wishes. Mackenzie Carpenter, a reporter for the *Pittsburgh Post-Gazette*, states that "no one [in Pennsylvania] actively searches for runaways, and even if they are found and put in group homes with a lot of supervision, there's no foolproof way to keep them there." Lack of police resources is also a problem, Carpenter adds, stating that "because the police have their hands full trying to solve crimes, they tend to consider runaway teenagers a low priority."[49] Though some people believe that it is better not to arrest runaways as if they were criminals, many family members and other people who care about these teens are unhappy about receiving little help from the law when it comes to locating their children.

Girls more than boys

Although teens who run away from home are a widely diverse group, there is a tendency for law-enforcement officials to divide them into two large classifications when arresting and charging them as runaways: girls and boys. According to R. Barri Flowers, runaway girls are more likely to be arrested than runaway boys. In 1998, for example, 68,170 girls were arrested for running away, while 48,919 boys were arrested for the same offense. There are a few reasons why these numbers differ so much. It appears girls are more likely than boys to run away from home. Also, male runaways often get caught while involved in more serious criminal offenses and are not classified as runaways upon arrest.

Police discretion is another factor in more teenage girls than boys being arrested as runaways. A law-enforcement

Runaway boys are far less likely to be arrested than runaway girls.

officer who knows that a girl is guilty of a more serious criminal offense may feel that arresting her as a runaway may get her out of a dangerous situation. For example, author Lillian Ambrosino notes that young female prostitutes "suspected to be unwillingly in the grip of a pimp, will sometimes be arrested only as runaways—a far lesser violation."[50]

When the law gets involved

The law often gets involved in cases of runaway teens when parents or caretakers ask for help to locate and return their children. Flowers notes that "according to the National Incidence Studies, an estimated 40 percent of police involvement in runaway cases results from reports of runaway children by parents or guardians."[51]

Aside from parental notification about a runaway, other factors are also considered when police decide how to handle a missing child who is suspected of running away. For instance, recent photographs of the teen and names and contact information of his or her close friends are used in the search. The more information officers have about the runaway, the better their chances are for finding the teenager. Police tend to act quickly if they believe there is a serious threat to a child's safety. As Flowers comments, "In most police agencies, reports of missing children who are very young or feared victims of kidnapping or foul play are given high priority."[52] In some cases, if no immediate danger against the teen seems likely, the police, who have other responsibilities and cases to solve, may not feel it necessary to intervene and may refer the youth's family to a social service agency.

Law enforcement officials who pass these cases onto social workers often do little to help the situation. Social workers who are assigned to work with runaways may often face obstacles and restraints similar to police officers. They often work with several youths at one time, and when one of these teens decides to leave home, social workers may not have the time to roam the streets in search of him or her.

The law also gets involved in the life of a runaway when that teen is charged with participation in criminal offenses such as prostitution or drug violations (buying, selling, or using illegal substances). Curfew and loitering violations are among other reasons that runaways may get arrested. These types of criminal behaviors are known by police as runaway-related offenses because they are activities often associated with those teens. Flowers offers the following statistics regarding these types of arrests:

> In 1998, persons under eighteen were arrested most often for runaway-related offenses. Over 146,000 persons under eighteen were arrested in the United States for drug abuse violations, more than 136,000 for curfew and loitering law violations, over 111,000 for liquor law violations, and more than 90,000 for vandalism. Though not all of these arrests were of runaway youth, studies show that there is a strong correlation between running away and certain offenses. Other runaway-related offenses that juveniles are arrested for include drunkenness, disorderly conduct, and prostitution. . . . Prostitution-related offenses are most often associated with youth who run away and are without food, adequate clothing, shelter, or other basic needs.[53]

Though many kids living on the streets are arrested as runaways, it is even more common for them to be arrested or detained for runaway-related offenses. This is especially true for push-outs and throwaways. Because the police are never notified that these teens are missing, they are unaware of their status, and many of these youths, particularly males, end up arrested for offenses other than running away.

When arrested, a runaway teen has the same rights as an adult, such as the right to remain silent (not say anything that would put him or her in further jeopardy with the law) and the right to legal counsel. Most runaways, however, since they are young offenders, are not tried in the same court as adult offenders. When a runaway's case goes to trial, that teen usually goes to juvenile court. Often runaways will either have to serve jail time or will be put on probation, which allows them to avoid prison while the police monitor their behavior. Some runaways who commit crimes will only be given a warning. All runaways apprehended for illegal activity, however, must face the possibility of being returned to the home from which they have fled. They also may be placed in foster homes if authorities view their home an unfit environment.

Those who try to help runaways

Some states have laws against helping teenagers on the run. The law is intended to protect the runaway from people who wish to harm rather than help them. According to William Young, commissioner of Social and Rehabilitation Services in Vermont, there are two kinds of people who

Police officers play a major role in determining how best to handle runaway teens.

Arrested teenagers have the same rights as adults, including the right to remain silent and the right to an attorney.

harbor runaways: There are those with "misguided good intentions," such as friends who provide runaways with food and shelter, and those "who harbor a runaway in order to prey on them," said Young.[54] The law is meant to protect teen runaways from predatory adults and to help parents and authorities locate the teens and return them home.

Some people view this law as problematic, especially for teens who are trying to flee abusive homes. Workers in shelters, halfway houses, and health care facilities are concerned that this law limits the amount of aid they can offer a runaway in crisis. These places are set up to help homeless youth, not to prey on them, but the fear of being charged with harboring a runaway (which can in some states lead to jail time) can often lead the workers in these facilities to deny young people the care they need, whether physical or emotional. What can happen in such a situation is that many homeless teens will refuse to seek out the help they need, even when seriously ill or pregnant, because the place they turn to could end up sending them back to an abusive home.

In spite of laws that some believe can hamper the effectiveness of social service agencies who wish to help runaways, there are always options for teens who need assistance. Though many teens feel their situation is desperate and that there is no hope for them once they leave home, that is certainly not the case. If a runaway decides that he or she is ready to seek help to get off the streets, that teen stands a better chance of avoiding conflicts with the law and staying out of life-threatening situations.

5

Help for Runaways

THOUGH THE LIFE of a homeless runaway is fraught with many dangers and risks—beatings, rape, drug and alcohol abuse, health problems, and in some cases, the possibility of arrest and detainment—there are options for those teens who are ready to ask for help. Many cities provide shelters and other programs designed to get kids off the streets and to help them begin to lead productive lives. Similar to the health care organizations that try to help kids, these programs attempt to assist homeless youths without passing judgment on them or expecting them to have parental permission in order to receive aid. Because of this, teens are often more likely to turn to these alternative programs, which do not attempt to force them back into their homes of origin or foster homes if these environments are considered unsafe.

Though these programs are not affiliated with law enforcement or conventional social service agencies, many of them are funded by the government. Under the Runaway and Homeless Youth Program, which was established by the Juvenile Justice and Delinquency Prevention Act, Congress has offered financial support to programs that assist runaways since 1974.

Aware that the number of runaways was increasing, Congress became concerned about the need for temporary shelter and counseling services, and believed such programs "would alleviate the problems of these youths, reunite them with their families, help them resolve intrafamily problems, strengthen family relationships, and stabilize living conditions."[55] Many of these programs have, in fact, been successful. The services funded under the Runaway and Homeless Youth Program include street outreach, basic or walk-in centers (shelters), and transitional living programs, which now operate in hundreds of communities across the country.

Runaways must admit they need help

Before a runaway is able to obtain any help, that teen must realize he or she is in need of it, and must make a commitment to improving his or her situation. Once a runaway is willing to admit he or she needs help, the teenager

Obtaining help from various programs and services can help many runaways to turn their lives around.

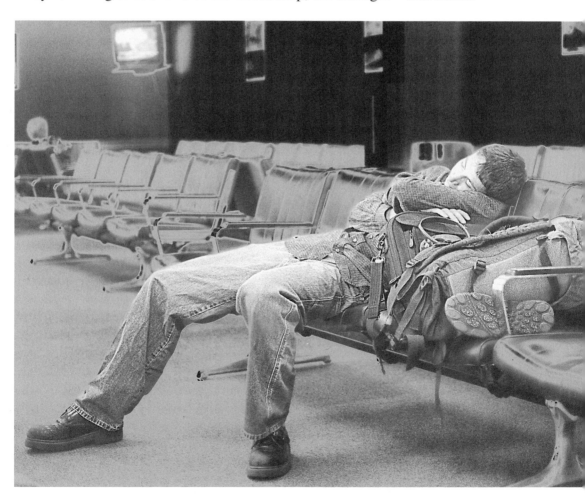

can turn to one of the many shelters nationwide, particularly in big cities. These programs, however, often have a set of rules that runaways are expected to follow, and some teens resist the idea of having to behave according to the programs' guidelines. For a teen willing to accept the rules, however, there is definite hope. Robert McGarvey, author of "Runaways: Children of the Night," says that these alternative places provide a variety of services such as

> shelter, food, job training, psychological counseling, and even . . . schooling. The programs impose rules: no drugs, alcohol or sex, and the kids must be willing to work. "The rules keep some kids out," admitted Teresa DeCrescenzo of the Homeless Youth Project, "but, without rules, we'd help nobody."[56]

The services these programs offer can help runaways turn their lives around. First, though, runaways have to become aware that these programs exist.

Street outreach

Street outreach is a type of program found most often in large cities, where runaways may be unaware of the assistance that is available to them. Rather than expecting runaways to search for assistance, these programs bring information about their services directly to the teens. Outreach workers comb the streets in search of homeless youths. They let them know about the services which are offered to keep them safe and healthy and tell them about programs created to help them improve their circumstances. These workers try to link runaways to health facilities, for both physical and mental conditions, and to other resources for counseling and more support. A major aim in outreach is to urge homeless kids to seek safety at local shelters.

Project Safe Place, a service of YMCA, is a program that offers outreach services to runaway youths. The workers at Project Safe Place offer counseling, shelter, and other resources. This program advertises its existence with bright yellow and black "Safe Place" signs, which are placed in the areas designated as Safe Place sites. These sites include businesses, community buildings, and buses, and any youth in need of assistance can simply walk in and speak to an employee, who will then put them in touch with the appropriate agencies.

This program has served a large number of homeless runaways. As of June 2002, help had been provided to 59,750 youths at Safe Place sites, and 52,519 kids had received counseling because of this program. Across the country, 11,669 Safe Place facilities were in operation. Though other outreach programs do exist, Project Safe Place is one of the more prominent and successful of its kind.

Basic or walk-in centers

Basic or walk-in centers, also known as shelters, help kids get off the streets as well. According to Peter Slavin, author of "Life on the Run, Life on the Streets," these centers "offer short-term shelter, food, clothing, and medical assistance as well as counseling to reunify families when possible and appropriate. If it is not, staff try to place a young person elsewhere or prepare him or her to live independently."[57] Temporary assistance at a shelter can often be the first step in helping a teen get off the streets.

Life in a shelter varies depending on each particular facility. In some shelters, especially those used for temporary housing, everyone eats and sleeps in the same room. These shelters can often be found in schools or churches. The room is filled with several cots or beds, to which the residents are assigned on a nightly basis. Other shelters are set up in hotels or residences, where whole families can stay together and enjoy a little more privacy than one-room facilities allow. Even in hotels and residences, however, people often have to share bathrooms and kitchen areas with other residents. Other shelters are built specifically for the homeless. Teen runaways living on their own are more likely to end up in one-room facilities.

There are many benefits for homeless people who choose to live in shelters, but there are drawbacks as well. All shelters, whether short-term or long-term, offer people a warm place to sleep. Many offer meals donated from food

Shelters provide short-term medical care and lodging for needy individuals or families.

pantries or prepared in soup kitchens. Medical care and counseling are available at some shelters as well. Hotels and residences often have a room set aside for kids, where they can play and work on their schoolwork with a tutor.

But no matter what kinds of assistance the shelter provides, it is still a temporary living arrangement. In fact, many one-room shelters are closed during the day, so runaways and homeless people are forced to leave in the morning and return in the evening. Sometimes the shelter is already full when they return, and they have to find somewhere else to sleep for the night.

Violence and crime can also be problems in a shelter. Emotions can run high, which can result in violent behavior among the residents. Mentally ill residents may also behave violently and erratically. To protect themselves and their belongings, many people who live in shelters wear their shoes to bed and keep their personal belongings close at hand to avoid losing these items to a thief. But in spite of these problems, teen runaways often find shelters to be a good alternative to living on the streets, where they are unlikely to find even a warm place to sleep.

The Children's Aid Society of West Texas runs a teen shelter that allows children from ages ten to seventeen to stay up to ninety days on a voluntary basis. By providing the teens a place to stay and assuring them that no one will hurt them while under their care, the shelter workers are often able to establish trust between themselves and the runaways. As soon as possible, someone contacts their parents or guardians, letting them know that their child is all right.

Many kids end up leaving and returning to the shelter several times before deciding to stay the full ninety days. This is fairly typical behavior for youths who already mistrust adults. They may not feel ready to accept help, or they may not feel prepared to follow the rules of the shelter. Though the shelter workers do not mind if it takes runaways time to decide if the program is right for them, once they do move in for a ninety-day stretch, the workers expect them to participate in a number of counseling sessions throughout the week. According to writer Amy Burgess, "Kids staying at the shelter go through individual counseling once a week, family counseling once a week and group counseling with the other shelter residents five times a week."[58] In other words, teens must be ready to commit to improving their circumstances while staying at the shelter.

Short-term programs offered by shelters can often be very helpful for teens who have only recently left home.

But for teens with long-term problems, programs cannot improve the environments from which the runaways have fled by simply offering family intervention and counseling services. Many of these facilities allow runaways to stay for only fifteen days, and this is often not enough time to address the serious problems the youths must face. When they do not have the time to make real progress in dealing with their issues, they often abandon the idea of seeking help altogether. Sometimes these kids will return for help in the future, but many of these programs are not equipped to deal with all of their problems.

Transitional living

If short-term programs cannot adequately help a runaway, he or she can try programs geared toward longer-term solutions. These programs, called transitional living programs, are often ideal for homeless youth between the ages of sixteen and twenty-one who have exhausted short-term options. These programs provide the youths—some of whom are single parents—with long-term, temporary housing and access to services that will better help them achieve independence. Programs that provide transitional living facilities allow runaway teens to stay in communal or other types of lodging while they work toward getting on their feet.

Bridge Over Troubled Waters, in Boston, is an example of an agency that provides transitional living opportunities to runaways. Considered a model program because of its remarkable success, Bridge also provides outreach and other types of services. According to writer Peter Slavin, it offers "school, a transitional day program, a medical van, a dental clinic, substance abuse counseling, family work and advocacy, and a pre-employment program."[59] Since Bridge is not a shelter, the facility has no beds to offer runaway and homeless teens. Instead, it hosts runaways in one of two ways: One program puts kids up for a night or two in the homes of local families. This program serves about two thousand kids a year. A second program provides housing for thirty-four young people—including single mothers—in communal homes or apartments under

Youth programs unable to adequately assess and deal with the issues of runaways can drive teens to return to the streets.

Bridge's transitional living service. Transitional living programs such as Bridge not only help get kids off the streets, they also help them to attain eventual independence.

Crisis hotlines

Aside from shelters and other support programs, there are organizations that provide valuable services to teenagers who hope to return home, to find an alternative place to

Crisis hotlines provide immediate assistance and support to runaways.

stay, or to seek counseling. Many of these organizations provide hotlines so that teens in trouble can contact them any time of the day or night when they are in need of help. For example, a teen may call a crisis hotline immediately after running away if he or she needs the location of the nearest shelter. Teenagers may also call after experiencing violence in the home and ask for help in accessing the appropriate services to take them out of a dangerous situation. The calls and services are free of charge, and the teens are under no obligation to follow the advice or suggestions of the trained volunteers who accept their calls.

The National Runaway Switchboard (NRS), a federally funded program, offers such a crisis hotline for teens in need. The organization accepts anonymous calls from teenagers and talks to them confidentially about their problems in a constructive manner. NRS attempts to offer practical advice concerning ways to get off the streets and advises its callers of nearby agencies that offer shelter and/or counseling services. Because of its comprehensive database, the organization is able to help teens find these services in virtually any part of the country. The NRS also accepts calls and provides help for family and friends of runaway teens, acknowledging that a teen's actions can affect many people.

The NRS is available twenty-four hours a day, and it offers a wide array of free services to its callers. The people who answer the phones—the "liners," as they are nicknamed—give callers someone to talk to when they feel they have nowhere else to turn. The liners listen intently and suggest different options for the youths to explore. Callers are referred to any type of service they may need, such as those that provide food, shelter, or other types of support, and the teens in crisis are urged to report abuse or assault to the appropriate authorities.

As a part of their services to family and friends, the NRS will convey messages to runaways from the people in their lives who care about them, as well as serve as mediators during phone conversations. As their website states, "A call to the National Runaway Switchboard can begin the process of getting off the streets and to a safe place."[60] Hotlines such as the NRS offer teens and those who care about them a place to turn for the support they need during a difficult time.

Another alternative program, called Home Free, provides runaway teens with free one-way transportation between any two points in the continental United States. Runaways between the ages of twelve and eighteen who use this service call the National Runaway Switchboard. The NRS then verifies the teen's status as a runaway. Once they have made this verification, the NRS contacts Greyhound Lines, Inc., to make the necessary arrangements. A service agency, the police, or someone at a shelter can also contact NRS on behalf of the runaway to help him or her obtain a free ride home.

Although the NRS and Greyhound Lines, Inc., are not the only organizations which work to help runaway teens deal with their problems or return home, they are two of the most prominent. However, with these services as well as others, teens on the run need to make the decision to seek assistance on their own. If they are not ready to be helped, then none of the services will be useful.

The importance of aftercare

Once a runaway has accepted that he or she needs help and has utilized immediate services such as hotlines, shelters, and other programs, ongoing, long-term support is often necessary to ensure that these youths are able to maintain a safe and productive lifestyle off the streets. Many of the organizations that provide shelter and support for runaway teens will also provide what is called aftercare. Aftercare services, such as individual or family counseling, are provided for the teen in order to keep him or her from becoming a runaway again. Continued contact with social service agencies also helps in this effort because the agencies can keep abreast of the teen's progress once returned home or moved into an alternative environment. For many teens, simply knowing that there are people concerned about their livelihood who

are checking in on them makes the decision to stay off the streets that much easier.

Though aftercare services help many teens resolve problems with their families and within themselves, they cannot help in every circumstance. These services, for example, cannot help teens with many stressful but common problems concerning school and finances. Families who suffer from such troubles often continue to experience difficulties that could lead teens to take to the streets once again. The long-term support offered by aftercare may not be able to solve all the issues these youths and their families face, but they can help them to better deal with these issues and to get through the hard times with their relationships intact.

Aftercare services offer counseling and long-term solutions to homeless and runaway youths.

6

Alternatives and Prevention

As IMPORTANT AS runaway and post-runaway support is, programs which help keep teens from running away in the first place are perhaps even more essential. A teen in need of help does not have to run away in order to seek assistance. Also, a parent or guardian with a child at risk of running away does not need to wait until something drastic occurs before looking for ways to solve the problems they are having at home. There are many options that can help prevent teens from running away, and many alternatives for the teen who believes that leaving home is the only answer.

What many teens and their parents need are runaway prevention programs to help keep problems from getting out of control. The troubles some teens are facing in school and in their homes can be dangerous and difficult for them and their families to handle on their own. Teens living in abusive households, for example, are often unaware of the options that exist to protect them and so believe that running is their only option. However, there are alternatives.

Foster care, group homes, halfway houses, and other substitute care placements can be good options for kids whose home lives are intolerable due to abuse or neglect. According to the Illinois Department of Children and Family Services, these alternative homes, however, "are not intended as permanent living arrangements for the child, but as a core service to protect the child while the ultimate goal of returning the child home or developing another permanent living situation is pursued."[61] The idea is to provide the youth with a stable environment in a homelike setting within his or her community. The time away from home is meant to be used productively by both the teen and the parents, who can take the opportunity to think about the problems they have been experiencing as a family and figure out ways to solve them.

Foster care and other temporary homes

The most recognized form of substitute housing for at-risk kids is foster care. Foster homes exist to provide children with a safe place to live or as alternative homes when kids are having trouble working problems out with their

Foster care homes provide children and teens with a safe and productive living environment.

families. Many children in the foster care system have been removed from their homes, and the need to place them in a different environment—even a temporary one—can often be urgent. There is a wide range of reasons as to why a teen would need to be placed in a foster home. For example, the teenager may be dealing with neglect or violence within his or her home, and it may be necessary to relocate the youth to ensure his or her safety. The teen may also suffer from health or emotional problems that the parents are unable to handle. If the parents are unwilling or unable to provide a secure environment for their child, a foster home situation can often be an ideal option.

Foster homes are not the same as adoptive homes. When a child or teen is adopted, it means that he or she is now a legal and permanent member of that family. Some kids are adopted as infants, while others are much older before they are placed in an adoptive home. The reasons for being offered for adoption vary. In some situations, the biological (natural) parents decide that they do not have the ability or resources (such as adequate money or food) to raise their child, so they allow the state to find that child an appropriate new home. In other cases, the state may deem the parents unfit to care for a child because of serious abuse of alcohol or drugs or violence in the home.

Children often end up in foster homes for the same reasons they are adopted, but the main difference is that foster homes are temporary living arrangements. A child may reside in a foster home for as little as twenty-four hours or for as long as several years. The foster family is legally accountable for the youth, as well as responsible for feeding, clothing, and providing emotional and physical support for that child. Though a child or teen could eventually be adopted by his or her foster parents. this is not always the case. In fact, some kids move from one foster home to another or from a foster home to their original home and then back to another foster home, until the state is satisfied that the best living environment has been found.

Though most foster homes are nurturing environments for young children and adolescents, some of these places can be unsafe. All foster parents are screened for things such as serious health problems (which may hinder an adult's ability to adequately care for a child), substance abuse problems, and a criminal past. They also must go through long and rigorous training before being allowed to care for a foster child. In spite of the extensive preparation they receive, some foster parents still are not prepared to be caretakers, and they too end up being abusive or neglectful of the child.

Foster families may be relatives or friends of the teenager, a situation that can be advantageous because the teen knows whom he or she is living with. But more likely, the youth will end up living with people who have been trained to become official foster parents. After spending some time in a foster home, a youth may be placed with an adoptive family if that child's home is still deemed unsafe.

Halfway houses are another form of temporary homes that can serve as alternatives to running away. Many halfway houses exist as havens for people recovering from alcohol and drug abuse problems, or those who are transitioning out of prison and back into society. However, there are many halfway houses that serve potential runaways and troubled youth. A halfway house provides the teen with a place to stay while trying to work things out at home or while trying to find new living arrangements.

While most shelters provide food and a place to sleep to almost anyone who drops in, halfway houses often have waiting lists of people who would like to use their services. Social service agencies are often involved in placing teens in these environments. Temporary housing such as halfway houses and foster homes, as well as shelters and transitional living environments, gives an at-risk youth options other than running away and becoming a victim of the streets.

Possible warning signs

When a teenager decides to run away from home, it is usually not a spontaneous decision. Often that teen has

A lack of communication among family members causes some teens to feel isolated and hopeless, increasing their chances of running away.

been considering running away as a solution to his or her problems for quite some time. The Youth Crisis Center (YCC), based in Jacksonville, Florida, believes that young people who may be planning an escape often display certain behaviors, which may be noticeable by the parents, siblings, or close friends. The YCC staff members suggest that it can be sometimes difficult to tell if a teen is going through serious turmoil or if he or she is simply experiencing typical adolescent problems, but they also think that teens at risk for running away exhibit warning signs, which would likely come in clusters if a real problem is evident.

The YCC cites changes in sleep pattern such as insomnia or sleeping too much, as as well as signs of frequent fatigue, as indicators of potential trouble. Withdrawal from family, rejection from or fights with friends, and problems in school (such as failing grades, skipping classes, and getting in trouble with teachers or the principal) are other possible signs. Family traumas such as death or divorce can also sometimes lead a teen to feel anxious and depressed. The YCC believes that parents need to discuss these problems with their kids, and that if communication is already poor between teens and their parents, it may not be easy to open up a dialogue about what is going on. That is why more active forms of prevention are often necessary. If the relationship between a parent and a child is already weak, it may be time to seek counseling or some other form of outside intervention in order to keep the family together.

Organizations and prevention strategies

Just as there are organizations that help teens once they are on the streets, there are also organizations that offer aid to teens and their families in order to prevent kids from leaving home in the first place. The STAR program in West Texas, for example, offers people the intervention they need to help families in the early stages of conflict through counseling services. The STAR program provides training in coping skills and parenting skills and sponsors support groups and mentoring services. Though it is possible to work things out at home without the aid of organizations such as the STAR program, many troubled families find their services very helpful.

Some agencies use creative ways to educate teenagers about the risks of running away. Since many teens often respond better to their peers than to their parents or other adults, some programs put them in contact with mature teens who can relate to what they are going through in their lives. Their advice and help is often well received by young people who have trouble trusting adults.

One agency in Dane County, Wisconsin, pairs this peer mentoring strategy with theater to raise awareness among the youth regarding the dangers of living on the streets. Young adults and adolescents perform skits for their peers to help educate teens about serious issues such as drug use, HIV infection, family violence, and running away. Slavin notes that "the skits, performed by past and present street kids and other teenagers, are followed by often animated discussions, with the actors staying in character."[62] The teen performers bring their act to churches, high schools, and places where runaway and homeless youth can be found. These theatrical productions have inspired many kids to seek counseling in order to discuss their own problems. Admitting they have a problem and asking for help are two important steps for teens who may be at risk for running away.

Another innovative program is the Covenant House Texas Community Runaway Prevention Initiative, which offers unique strategies to youth who are considered at risk of running away. Often guilty of delinquent or other negative behaviors, these teens are in need of some sort of intervention, and the Covenant House uses creative methods to reach them. They utilize discussion and role-playing techniques to teach these kids ways to handle school- or home-related problems. Topics discussed in their workshops include ways to manage their anger, how to resolve conflicts, self-esteem issues, and alcohol and drug prevention. When teens need further help, the Covenant House offers information and referrals that will help them find additional assistance.

Congress is working to prevent teens from running away

The U.S. government is becoming aware of the need to set up more organizations and agencies which can help keep kids from running away. A 2001 study authorized by Congress concluded that more services are needed to prevent teens from leaving home and to protect them if they do. Writer Peter Slavin says, "The study cited family preservation and support services, such as mediation and family counseling, to assist families at risk while young people are still in the home."[63] This study also stressed the

Because teen homelessness has become so widespread, the U.S. government is working to sponsor more family preservation services.

need for more outreach programs and early intervention for teens who have recently run away, and drop-in programs such as shelters and health clinics for those teens who have been living on the streets for awhile.

Since the release of this study's findings, more has been done by the government to work toward runaway prevention. In 2002, for example, November was declared the first-ever National Runaway Prevention Month. Together, the National Runaway Switchboard (NRS) and the National Network for Youth gave November this designation "in an effort to increase public awareness of the life circumstances of youth at risk of running away and the need for safe, healthy, and productive alternatives, resources, and supports for such youth and their families and communities."[64] People participated in a number of activities to commemorate the month and persuaded local television stations, radio stations, or newspapers to feature information about running away that shared ideas for prevention. Presentations concerning the dangers of living on the streets were given to youths in schools or community organizations. These activities raised awareness and educated the public regarding the many problems associated with running away.

The Conference on Missing, Exploited and Runaway Children

The government has made other efforts to inform people of the teen runaway problem. As a result of the many child abduction and murder cases that occurred in 2002, for example, President George W. Bush hosted the White House Conference on Missing, Exploited and Runaway Children. About six hundred people—law-enforcement officials, child advocates, and human service providers—met in Washington, D.C., to discuss the needs of at-risk youth. Attendees heard panel discussions on high-risk youth, including runaways and kids who are otherwise homeless.

The conference also discussed America's Missing Broadcast Emergency Response system, otherwise known as the AMBER alert. AMBER alert involves partnerships between police and local broadcasters to immediately notify the public in when a child has been abducted. When a child goes missing, electronic message boards on the country's highways flash information about the missing youth, the abductor, and/or the vehicle the child was last seen in.

The Bush administration has pledged $10 million toward developing AMBER training and education programs, maintaining the emergency alert systems through upgrades, and installing more message boards along roads.

The Bush administration has allocated $10 million to combat the problem of teen runaways.

AMBER ALERT
WHT 95 JEEP
NE LIC NDW242

Posted above many freeways, AMBER alert signs help authorities locate missing and runaway teens.

The Conference on Missing, Exploited and Runaway Children helped to raise people's awareness about the serious dangers faced by many of the nation's children and adolescents, and it also provided an opportunity for people to consider ways to prevent youths from ending up on the streets.

Staying off the streets

The efforts put forth by the government and other organizations to help prevent teens from running away are often useful to youths and their families. For many kids, however, the struggle to remain in a home where they feel extremely unhappy, or where they believe their safety is threatened, is a difficult one, even with assistance from others. Prevention and alternative programs may not work for every teen, and in spite of the amount of education, counseling, and awareness training they may receive, many will still end up running away. The same can be said for a lot of teens who are already on the streets. Though a wide variety of services exist to help runaway youths, even those who take advantage of what these programs have to offer may not be able to change their situations for the better.

There *are* many people, however, who benefit from prevention and alternative programs. Teens willing to admit they need help and parents and guardians who are committed to helping their kids and to keeping their families intact are the most likely to successfully prevent a runaway situation. Continued counseling and educational services offered by the government and other organizations can help alleviate the problems potential runaways are facing in their homes and can give their families the support and education they need to help maintain a caring and nurturing environment. Through these programs, many young adults may learn that they have options other than running away, and they may ultimately realize that becoming a runaway is not the only answer, and that staying off the streets is the best decision for them to make.

Notes

Introduction

1. Laurie Schaffner, *Teenage Runaways: Broken Hearts and "Bad Attitudes."* New York: Haworth Press, 1999, p. 5.

Chapter 1: Who Are Teen Runaways and Why Do They Run?

2. Schaffner, *Teenage Runaways*, p. 10.

3. Peter Slavin, "Life on the Run, Life on the Streets," *Children's Voice*, Child Welfare League of America, July 2001. www.cwla.org.

4. Anonymous, "I Am a Runaway," *Runaway Lives: Personal Stories and Reflections by Runaways and Their Families*, Penn State–Lehigh Valley, January 17, 2002. www.an.psu.edu.

5. Quoted in "A Critical Look at the Foster Care System," *Lifting the Veil: Examining the Child Welfare, Foster Care and Juvenile Justice Systems*, July 13, 1998. http://home.rica.net.

6. Jeffrey Artenstein, *Runaways: In Their Own Words.* New York: RGA, 1990, p. xv.

7. BabyJill, "BabyJill Is My Street Name, Because I Was so Young," *Runaway Lives*, April 29, 2002.

8. "Runaway Story," *Runaway Lives*, April 29, 2002.

9. "Being Out, Coming Home," *National Runaway Switchboard*, 2001. www.nrscrisisline.org.

10. Quoted in Robert McGarvey, "Runaways: Children of the Night," *American Legion Magazine*, 2002, SIRS (Social Issues Resources Series). www.sirs.com.

11. Quoted in McGarvey, "Runaways."

12. Artenstein, *Runaways*, p. xv.

13. Artenstein, *Runaways*, p. xv.

Chapter 2: Life on the Streets

14. BabyJill, "Baby Jill Is My Street Name."

15. Quoted in McGarvey, "Runaways."

16. Julia Gilden, "See How They Run," *In These Times*, January 1990, SIRS. www.sirs.com.

17. Quoted in Slavin, "Life on the Run, Life on the Streets."

18. Anonymous, "I Am a Runaway."

19. Slavin, "Life on the Run, Life on the Streets."

20. McGarvey, "Runaways."

21. McGarvey, "Runaways."

22. James A. Farrow, M.D., ed., "Health and Health Needs of Homeless and Runaway Youth: A Position Paper of the Society for Adolescent Medicine," *Journal of Adolescent Health*, 1992. www.adolescenthealth.org.

23. Dylan Foley and Andrea D'Asaro, "Girls and the Business of Sex: From Senegal to Philadelphia, Girls Getting Out of 'the Life,'" *On the Issues: The Progressive Woman's Quarterly*, Summer 1997, SIRS. www.sirs.com.

24. "Escape from Sexual Exploitation," *The Paul & Lisa Program*. www.paulandlisa.org.

25. "Escape from Sexual Exploitation," *The Paul & Lisa Program*.

26. Quoted in Foley and D'Asaro, "Girls and the Business of Sex."

27. Foley and D'Asaro, "Girls and the Business of Sex."

28. Farrow, "Health and Health Needs of Homeless and Runaway Youth."

29. Quoted in McGarvey, "Runaways."

30. Quoted in Gilden, "See How They Run."

31. Quoted in McGarvey, "Runaways."

32. "Facts & Stats & Definitions," *The Paul & Lisa Program.* www. paulandlisa.org.

33. Quoted in Rod Minott, "Teen Runaways," PBS, May 14, 1996. www.pbs.org.

Chapter 3: Runaways Face Serious Health Risks

34. Trish Crawford, "Hanging Out in a Harsh City with a Growing Band of Street Kids," *Toronto Star*, March 4, 1995. SIRS. www.sirs.com.

35. Quoted in Trish Crawford, "Helping Hands for the Homeless," *Toronto Star*, March 5, 1995. SIRS. www.sirs.com.

36. Sabin Russell, "Haven for Youth with AIDS: New Tenderloin Center Provides Respite from Life on the Streets," *San Francisco Chronicle*, October 17, 1997, AEGIS. www.aegis.com.

37. Quoted in Gilden, "See How They Run."

38. Quoted in Gilden, "See How They Run."

39. Crawford, "Hanging Out in a Harsh City with a Growing Band of Street Kids."

40. June R. Wyman, "Drug Abuse Among Runaway and Homeless Youths Calls for Focused Outreach Solutions," National Institute on Drug Abuse, May/June 1997. www. drugabuse.gov.

41. Farrow, "Health and Health Needs of Homeless and Runaway Youth."

42. Michael G. Connor, Psy. D., "Understanding and Dealing with Conduct and Oppositional Disorders," *Oregon*

Counseling, December 4, 2002. www.oregoncounseling.org.

43. Farrow, "Health and Health Needs of Homeless and Runaway Youth."

44. Farrow, "Health and Health Needs of Homeless and Runaway Youth."

Chapter 4: Runaways and the Law

45. R. Barri Flowers, *Runaway Kids and Teenage Prostitution: America's Lost, Abandoned, and Sexually Exploited Children.* Westport, CT: Greenwood Press, 2001, pp. 35–36.

46. Paul Ludwig, "The Laws Regarding a Parent's Right to Place and/or Transport Their Child to a Program," *Teen Rescue.* www.teenrescue.com.

47. Lillian Ambrosino, *Runaways.* Boston: Beacon Press, 1971, p. 31.

48. Amy Burgess, "Teen Shelter Gives Runaways Protection," *Times Record News,* October 17, 1999. www.uway-wftx.org.

49. Mackenzie Carpenter, "There's No Law Against Youngsters Who Won't Stay at Home," *Pittsburgh Post-Gazette,* January 26, 2003. www.post-gazette.com.

50. Ambrosino, *Runaways,* p. 33.

51. Flowers, *Runaway Kids and Teenage Prostitution,* p. 36.

52. Flowers, *Runaway Kids and Teenage Prostitution,* pp. 36–37.

53. Flowers, *Runaway Kids and Teenage Prostitution,* p. 35.

54. Quoted in "Three Charged Under New Runaway Law," *Times Argus Online,* February 3, 2002. www.timesargus.com.

Chapter 5: Help for Runaways

55. Deborah Bass, *Helping Vulnerable Youths: Runaway &*

Homeless Adolescents in the United States. Washington, DC: NASW Press, 1992, p. 14.

56. Quoted in McGarvey, "Runaways."

57. Slavin, "Life on the Run, Life on the Streets."

58. Burgess, "Teen Shelter Gives Runaways Protection."

59. Slavin, "Life on the Run, Life on the Streets."

60. "Services for Runaway Youth," *National Runaway Switchboard*, 2002. www.nrscrisisline.org.

Chapter 6: Alternatives and Prevention

61. "Foster Care Brochure," *Illinois Department of Children and Family Services.* www.state.il.us.

62. Slavin, "Life on the Run, Life on the Streets."

63. Slavin, "Life on the Run, Life on the Streets."

64. "Washington Hotline," *New England Network for Child, Youth & Family Services*, October 7, 2002. www.nenetwork.org.

Organizations to Contact

The following organizations provide help and information for teen runaways and their families.

Child Welfare League of America
50 F Street NW, 6th Floor
Washington, DC 20001-2085
Phone: 202-638-2952
Fax: 202-638-4004
Website: www.cwla.org

This nonprofit organization helps millions of abused and neglected children and their families each year.

Children of the Night
14530 Sylvan Street
Van Nuys, CA 91411
Phone: 800-551-1800
Phone: 818-808-4474
Website: www.childrenofthenight.org

Children of the Night offers support services to homeless and runaway youth involved in prostitution and pornography.

The Covenant House
Phone: 800-999-9999
Website: www.covenanthouse.org

This privately funded childcare agency provides shelter and a wide range of other services to homeless and runaway youth across the United States. Their hotline—Nineline— offers over-the-phone counseling to teens in trouble and their families.

Family and Youth Services Bureau (FYSB)
U.S. Department of Health and Human Services
P.O. Box 1882
Washington, DC 20013
Phone: 202-205-8102
Fax: 202-260-9333
Website: www.acf.dhhs.gov/programs/fysb

FYSB provides national leadership on issues involving youth. This organization also provides services and opportunities for at-risk youth, including runaways and the homeless.

National Runaway Switchboard (NRS)
3080 N. Lincoln Avenue
Chicago, IL 60657
Phone: 800-621-4000
Phone: 773-880-9860
Fax: 773-929-5150
E-mail: info@nrscrisisline.org
Website: www.nrscrisisline.org

The NRS offers a wide range of services through their hotline and website. These services include referrals to other organizations for food, shelter, and other resources; connections to authorities to report abuse or assault; and a message service which sends information from the runaway to the family or vice versa. Through their partnership with Greyhound Lines, Inc., NRS also provides a way for teens to return home.

Teen Rescue
P.O. Box 1463
Corona, CA 92878-1463
Phone: 800-494-2200
Fax: 909-549-0585
E-mail: teenrescue@aol.com
Website: www.teenrescue.com

This organization provides support services for the parents and families of at-risk youth and helps locate missing and runaway kids.

YMCA National Safe Place
2400 Crittenden Drive
Louisville, KY 40217
Phone: 888-290-7233
Phone: 502-635-3660
Fax: 502-635-1443
E-mail: nationalsafeplace@ymcalouisville.org
Website: www.safeplaceservices.org

Project Safe Place, sponsored by the YMCA National Safe Place program, provides youth in crisis with immediate access to help and support services. Designated Safe Place sites display the Safe Place yellow and black logo.

For Further Reading

Julie Parker, *Everything You Need to Know About Living in a Shelter.* New York: Rosen, 1995. Parker discusses the many reasons a young person may end up living in a shelter, including running away. Issues such as how to cope with feelings about shelter life and the possible problems faced in such an environment are addressed. Includes photographs.

Renee C. Rebman, *Runaway Teens.* Berkeley Heights, NJ: Enslow, 2001. The author allows teen runaways to tell their own tales about life on the streets. Many of these stories have happy endings as the kids turn to different organizations for help.

Gail Stewart, *The Other America: The Homeless.* San Diego: Lucent Books, 1996. Four stories about life as a homeless person are presented. Marylin's story, for example, illustrates how a cycle of running away as a teen can lead to homelessness as an adult. Black-and-white photographs are included.

Gail Stewart and Natasha Frost (photographer), *Teen Runaways.* San Diego: Lucent Books, 1997. Stewart begins by providing basic information regarding the facts about teen runaways, then focuses each chapter on a true runaway story. Ways to get involved in helping teen runaways and suggestions for further reading are also included.

Ellen Switzer, *Anyplace But Here: Young, Alone, and Homeless: What to Do*. New York: Atheneum, 1992. The author examines the issue of teen runaways, including who they are, why they choose to leave home, and where they go. She also provides information regarding health concerns for runaways and what is involved in the decision to get off the streets.

Clare Tattersall, *Drugs, Runaways, and Teen Prostitution*. New York: Rosen, 1998. Tattersall discusses the risks teen runaways face, from prostitution to the use of illegal substances.

Works Consulted

Books

Lillian Ambrosino, *Runaways*. Boston: Beacon Press, 1971. A useful though dated resource that describes the typical runaway and provides information regarding how runaways survive on the streets, cope with health problems, and deal with loneliness. One chapter offers advice to children and their parents. Black-and-white photographs are included.

Jeffrey Artenstein, *Runaways: In Their Own Words*. New York: RGA, 1990. In 1988 the author interviewed several young runaways while volunteering at the Los Angeles Youth Network. In this volume, he allows some of these runaways to speak for themselves, providing their true and often harrowing stories about life on the streets. He begins each chapter with a description of the runaway who is offering his or her story.

Deborah Bass, *Helping Vulnerable Youths: Runaway & Homeless Adolescents in the United States*. Washington, DC: NASW Press, 1992. With social workers in mind, Bass outlines information about runaways, including the characteristics and needs of vulnerable youth and the federal programs in place for these youths. She also offers recommendations for ways to better serve runaway and homeless kids.

R. Barri Flowers, *Runaway Kids and Teenage Prostitution: America's Lost, Abandoned, and Sexually Exploited Children*. Westport, CT: Greenwood Press, 2001. In this excellent resource about teen runaways and prostitution, the author begins by outlining information about runaways such as why they run, how they cope with the law, and the perils they face on the street. He then discusses the dynamics of teenage prostitution, including the differences between boy prostitutes and girl prostitutes. Flowers also discusses the correlation between running away and becoming involved in prostitution.

Laurie Schaffner, *Teenage Runaways: Broken Hearts and "Bad Attitudes."* New York: Haworth Press, 1999. A former runaway, Schaffner attempts to make the plight of runaways clear by providing statistics and a history of the problem. She also offers theories about the emotional reasons teens run away, discussing issues such as defiance, conflict management, and the role of the family in the lives of runaways.

Internet Sources

"Being Out, Coming Home," *National Runaway Switchboard*, 2001. www.nrscrisisline.org.

Amy Burgess, "Teen Shelter Gives Runaways Protection," *Times Record News*, October 17, 1999. www.uway-wftx.org.

Mackenzie Carpenter, "There's No Law Against Youngsters Who Won't Stay at Home," *Pittsburgh Post-Gazette*, January 26, 2003. www.post-gazette.com.

Michael G. Connor, Psy.D, "Understanding and Dealing with Conduct and Oppositional Disorders," *Oregon Counseling*, December 4, 2002. www.oregoncounseling.org.

Trish Crawford, "Hanging Out in a Harsh City with a Growing Band of Street Kids," *Toronto Star*, March 4, 1995. SIRS. www.sirs.com.

Trish Crawford, "Helping Hands for the Homeless," *Toronto Star*, March 5, 1995. SIRS. www.sirs.com

"Escape from Sexual Exploitation," *The Paul & Lisa Program.* www.paulandlisa.org.

"Facts & Stats & Definitions," *The Paul & Lisa Program.* www.paulandlisa.org.

"A Critical Look at the Foster Care System," *Lifting the Veil: Examining the Child Welfare, Foster Care and Juvenile Justice Systems*, July 13, 1998. http://home.rica.net.

James A. Farrow, M.D., ed., "Health and Health Needs of Homeless and Runaway Youth: A Position Paper of the Society for Adolescent Medicine," *Journal of Adolescent Health*, 1992. www.adolescenthealth.org.

Dylan Foley and Andrea D'Asaro, "Girls and the Business of Sex: From Senegal to Philadelphia, Girls Getting out of 'the Life.'" *On the Issues: The Progressive Woman's Quarterly*, Summer 1997, SIRS. www.sirs.com.

"Foster Care," *Tennessee Anytime*, 2002, www.state.tn.us.

"Foster Care Brochure," *Illinois Department of Children and Family Services*. www.state.il.us.

Julia Gilden, "See How They Run," *In These Times*, January 1990, SIRS. www.sirs.com.

Michael Hedges, "Senators Push for Changes in Laws on Teen Runaways," *Peekaboo*, July 17, 1997. www.peekaboo.net.

"Holidays Time of Heightened Concern for Gay Runaways in San Francisco," CNN.com, November 29, 2000. www.cnn.com.

Melissa Korn, "County Homelessness Topic of Panel Talk," *Cornell Daily Sun*, November 7, 2002. cornelldailysun.com.

Paul Ludwig, "The Laws Regarding a Parent's Right to Place and/or Transport Their Child to a Program," *Teen Rescue*. www.teenrescue.com.

Robert McGarvey, "Runaways: Children of the Night,"

American Legion Magazine, 2002, SIRS. www.sirs.com.

Rod Minott, "Teen Runaways," PBS, May 14, 1996. www.pbs.org.

"Runaway Prevention Initiative," *Covenant House Texas*, www.covenanthousetx.org.

Sabin Russell, "Haven for Youth with AIDS: New Tenderloin Center Provides Respite from Life on the Streets," *San Francisco Chronicle*, October 17, 1997, AEGIS. www.aegis.com.

"Safe Place," *YMCA National Safe Place*, 2002. www.safeplaceservices.org.

"Services for Runaway Youth," *National Runaway Switchboard*, 2002. www.nrscrisisline.org.

Peter Slavin, "Life on the Run, Life on the Streets," *Children's Voice*, Child Welfare League of America, July 2001. www.cwla.org.

Paul Srubas, "Special Report: Laws Keep Some Pregnant Teens from Seeking Help," *Green Bay Press Gazette*, October 10, 2001, www.greenbaypressgazette.com.

"Study of Runaways Reveals Disturbing Data on Abuse, Mental Illness," *Newswise*, July 2, 2002. www.newswise.com.

"Three Charged Under New Runaway Law," *Times Argus Online*, February 3, 2002. www.timesargus.com.

"University of Nebraska–Lincoln Sociologists Conducting First Longitudinal Study of Runaway Teenagers." *Science Coalition*. www.sciencecoalition.org.

"Washington Hotline," *New England Network for Child, Youth & Family Services*, October 7, 2002. www.nenetwork.org.

June R. Wyman, "Drug Abuse Among Runaway and Homeless Youths Calls for Focused Outreach Solutions,"

National Institute on Drug Abuse, May/June 1997.
www.drugabuse.gov.

Websites

Greyhound Lines, Inc. (www.greyhound.com).

The Paul and Lisa Program (www.paulandlisa.org).

Runaway Lives: Personal Stories and Reflections by Runaways and Their Families. Penn Sate–Lehigh Valley (www.an.psu.edu/jkl1/runawaylives).

Index

abduction, 82
addiction, 18–19, 26, 30, 40
adolescents, 12, 26, 34, 76,
  79, 80
  see also teens
adoption, 76
aftercare, 72–73
agencies, 16, 18, 54, 77
AIDS, 33, 34, 39, 48
alcohol abuse, 18, 41, 43, 76
alternative programs, 75–77
AMBER alert, 82–83
Ambrosino, Lillian, 51, 57
America's Missing
  Broadcast Emergency
  Response system.
  See AMBER alert
anger, 54, 80
arrest, 49, 55, 57, 58
Artenstein, Jeffrey, 15, 19,
  20, 22
Assisted Care and After
  Care Facility, 48

BabyJill, 16, 17, 23
begging. *See* panhandle
Boston, 47, 68
Breault, Susan, 32
Bridge over Troubled
  Waters, 68, 70

broadcasters, 83
Burgess, Amy, 54, 67
Bush, George W., 82

cafeteria, 53
Canada, 50
Carpenter, Mackenzie, 55
ChildHope International, 30
Children of the Night, 18
Children's Aid Society, 54,
  67
chores, 51
churches, 65, 80
cocaine, 43
communication, 11
conduct disorder. *See* psy-
  chological disorders
Conference on Missing,
  Exploited and Runaway
  Children, 83–85
Congress, 62, 81
Connor, G. Michael, 44
Corona, California, 50
counseling, 64, 66, 67, 71,
  79, 80
Covenant House Texas
  Community Runaway
  Preventive Initiative, 80
crack, 43
Crawford, Trish, 38, 43

criminal acts, 29, 33, 49, 52
curfews, 51, 58
custody, 51

Dane County, Wisconsin, 80
D'Asaro, Andrea, 30, 33
DeCrescenzo, Teresa, 64
deliquents, 52
Department of Health and Human Services, 14
depression, 44, 45, 46
detention centers, 49, 55
drug abuse, 18–20, 33, 41, 43, 76
drug dealing, 29–30, 43, 49
dumpster diving. *See* trashing

ecstasy, 43
education, 33, 40, 53
emergency room, 46
Essex, California, 30
Ewert, Ruth, 38, 39

Farrow, James A., Dr. 30, 33, 44, 45, 46
fatigue, 79
Flowers, R. Barri, 49, 55, 58
food pantries, 66
foster care, 11, 15, 59, 75, 76, 77

garbage cans, 27
gay, 14, 17, 33
Gilden, Julia, 25

"Girls and the Business of Sex" (D'Asaro), 30
Greyhound Lines, Inc., 72
guardians, 9, 16, 47

halfway houses, 60, 74, 77
hallucinogens, 43
hazards, 22, 37
health insurance, 46
Hedman, Becca, 34
Hedman, Dennis, 34
heroin, 43
HIV, 33, 38, 40, 47, 80
Home Free, 72
homeless
    health care for, 44–48
    health risks of, 39–40
    safety of, 23–25
    shelters for, 65
    see also runaways
Homeless Youth Project, 64
homicide, 38
homosexuals, 14, 17
hotels, 65
hotlines, 12, 71, 72
hypertension, 40

Illinois Department of Children and Family Services, 74
inhalants, 43
insomnia, 79
Internet, 31

Jackson, Kevin, 25
Jacksonville, Florida, 79
juvenile court, 58

juvenile detention center, 49, 52, 54
Juvenile Justice and Delinquency Prevention Act, 62

Larkin Street Youth Services, 11, 42, 48
laws
  protective, 59–60
  runaways and, 49–51
  violations of, 58
L.A. Youth Network, 18
Lee, Lois, 18
lesbians, 14, 17, 33
"Life on the Run, Life on the Streets" (Slavin), 65
lifestyle, 38, 40
loitering, 58
Los Angeles, 23, 46, 47
Ludwig, Paul, 49

malnutrition, 27, 38
marijuana, 43
McGarvey, Robert, 25, 29, 34, 64
mediation, 71, 81
medical care, 53, 66
Melodie, 29
mental disorder, 14
minors, 32
motels, 25
mugging, 25

National Association of Social Workers, 14
National Incidence Studies, 37
National Institute of Drug Abuse (NIDA), 42, 43
National Network for Youth, 82
National Runaway Prevention Month, 82
National Runaway Switchboard (NRS), 12, 17, 71, 72, 82
New York, 23, 47
Nicholson, Luree, 18

Our Town Family Center, 26
outreach, 26, 47, 63, 64, 65, 68

panhandle, 8, 29
parents, 9, 16, 19, 47, 51, 55
Paul & Lisa Program, 30, 31, 32, 34
pedophiles, 31
peer mentoring, 80
peer pressure, 33
peers, 13, 39, 44, 80
Penn State–Lehigh Valley, 15
Pennsylvania State, 55
pimps, 32, 33, 34, 57
Pittsburgh Post-Gazette (newspaper), 55
police, 43, 47, 51, 57-58, 83
pornography, 11, 30, 31, 32
poverty, 14, 29
pregnancies, 38, 40, 42

prenatal care, 40–41
prisons, 49, 54, 58, 77
probation, 54, 58
Project Safe Place, 64, 65
prostitution, 11, 30–34, 49
psychological disorders,
  44–46
push-outs. *See* throwaways

Raider, 25, 27
rape, 8, 43, 62
Rocky, Marilyn, 30
role plays, 80
Runaway and Homeless
  Youth Program, 62, 63
Runaway Lives (website),
  14, 16, 26
runaways
  education of, 53
  exploitation of, 30–32
  foster care and, 15
  health problems of, 39–42
  independence of, 34
  insecurity of, 19, 25–26
  parents of, 17–20
  prevention programs for,
    79–80
  reasons of, for leaving,
    8–9, 13–14, 16
  statistics of, 12, 13, 23,
    55, 65
  suicide and, 44–46
  see also homeless
"Runaways: Children of the
  Night" (McGarvey), 64

San Francisco, 23, 47
Schaffner, Laurie, 8, 12

schools, 65, 80
Seattle, Washington, 47
sedatives, 43
sex, 30, 33, 38, 40, 41
sexual exploitation. *See*
  runaways, exploitation of
sexually transmitted dis-
  eases (STDs), 33, 38, 40,
  42, 47
shelters, 54, 64, 65, 66, 67,
  71
Slavin, Peter, 14, 27, 65,
  68, 80, 81
Social and Rehabilitation
  Services (Vermont), 59
social service agencies, 54,
  57, 61
squats, 25
STAR program, 79
status offender, 44
STDs. *See* sexually transmitted diseases
street life
  exploitation and, 30–32
  dangers of, 23, 25, 37
  risks of diseases in, 39,
    40
  survival of, 27–30
  violence of, 34–37
  see also runaways
suicide, 43, 44, 46
surrogate families, 26
Suthireung, Varee, 32
*Teenage Runaways: Broken
  Hearts and "Bad
  Attitudes"* (Schaffner), 8
Teen Rescue, 49
teens, 18, 46, 49, 51, 58, 79

throwaways, 16, 17–18, 58
Times Record News (newspaper), 54
Toronto (Canada), 38, 43
transients, 25
trashing, 27
Tucson, Arizona, 26

University of Nebraska–Lincoln, 44
University of Washington, Seattle, 47

vandalism, 44, 58
Van Nuys, California, 18

Vermont, 59
victims, 43, 77
violence, 14, 43, 44, 67, 71, 76

walk-in centers, 63, 65
Washington, D.C., 82
website, 15, 17, 32, 34, 71
White House, 82
Wisconsin, 80

YMCA, 64
Young, William, 59, 60
Youth Crisis Center (YCC), 79

Picture Credits

About the Author

Christina Veladota earned her M.F.A. from the University of North Carolina at Greensboro and her Ph.D. from Ohio University, where she currently teaches writing courses and works as an editor for *Quarter After Eight: A Journal of Prose and Commentary*. Her poetry has appeared in several literary magazines, including *The Journal, Mid-American Review*, and *Ascent*. She is also the recipient of a 2003 Ohio Arts Council Individual Artist fellowship. This is her first publication with Lucent Books.